The
Three Ages
of the
Italian
Renaissance

The
Three Ages
of the
Italian
Renaissance

By Robert S. Lopez
Yale University

The University Press
of Virginia
Charlottesville

Richard Lectures for 1968–1969
University of Virginia

The University Press of Virginia
Copyright © 1970 by the Rector and Visitors
of the University of Virginia

First published 1970

Standard Book Number: 8139–0270–3
Library of Congress
Catalog Card Number: 75–94759
Printed in the United States of America

Frontispiece: The battle of Porta Camollia
(miniature of the Tavole di Biccherna,
Archivio di Stato, Siena)
The initial letters are from *La historia
delle cose facte dallo invictissimo Duca
Francesco Sforza* by Giovanni Simoneta
(Milan: printed by Antonio Zarotto, 1490).

Acknowledgments

LET my first acknowledgment go to five differently youthful persons whose conversation has made my life more interesting: my sons, Michael and Larry; my wife, Claude; my brother, Guido; my mother, Sisa. The relentless drive of my mother makes me wonder whether she might not be the youngest of them all.

In the second place I would give credit at large for many suggestions I have received over the years, but can no longer trace back to their authors—friends and colleagues in many countries, students, books and sources dimly but steadily remembered. Even the most conscientious historian does not escape unconscious plagiarism when writing about problems that have long been on his mind.

More precisely, and in addition to the authors cited in the footnotes, I wish to thank Dr. Elizabeth Chase, of Yale University, and her colleagues at the Art Library, Helen Chillman and Yasuko Betchaku; Dr. Ubaldo Morandi, director of the Archivio di Stato of Siena; Count Silvio Piccinelli, president of the Ente per il Turismo of Bergamo; Dr. Gaetano Panazza, director of the Museum of Brescia; Dr. Giuliana Bologna, director of the Biblioteca Trivulziana of Milan; and my charming friends Stella Matalon and Luisa Zani, all of whom have assisted me in gathering illustrations. These are to be credited as follows: Color plate, Archivio di Stato, Siena; Plate IV, Ente per il Turismo, Bergamo; Plate VI, Biblioteca Trivulziana, Milan; Plates VII (top), IX, XI, Photographie Giraudon; Plates XIV and XV, Amici di Brera, Milan; Plate X, Kunsthistorisches Museum, Vienna; all other plates, Fratelli Alinari. Lastly, I want to express my gratitude to the University Press of Virginia, and more especially to the members of its staff, for giving my book their benevolent and intelligent care.

With the exception of one octave of Ariosto and one passage of Fracastoro, all translations from Renaissance authors (both prose and verse) are my own. To lighten my responsibility for possible misinterpretations, I ought to supply page references to the original texts; but how could I choose one of many equally acceptable editions of often reprinted, famous authors? At any rate, the Italian text of nearly all the poems can easily be found in at least one of two anthologies printed in England, the *Oxford Book of Italian Verse* and the *Penguin Book of Italian Verse*. Most prose excerpts, in somebody else's translation, have appeared in a good number of American source books of the Renaissance. It would be invidious to single out only one of several competent renderings.

R. S. L.

New Haven, Connecticut
October 1969

Contents

The
Three Ages
of the
Italian
Renaissance

I Ancestry

FELT somewhat uneasy when I read the three lectures that were the origin of this book in the Jeffersonian Renaissance surroundings of the University of Virginia. Even now, I am not fully reassured. Though I have never refrained from expressing my opinion about the Italian Renaissance, my main trade is medieval economic history. The dirty boots of the economist are notoriously unwelcome on the polished floors of humanistic mansions; rejection of the Middle Ages is imbedded in the very definition of the Renaissance. Will it be said that an economic historian discussing works of art is like a teetotaler prattling about wine, or that a medievalist cannot be fair to the Renaissance? I shall reply, in the mediocre Latin that humanists reproached to medieval writers, "primum vivere, deinde philosophari"; that is, artists have to eat, buildings need foundations, and while any style can rest on any foundation, size and solidity depend largely on the economic groundwork. Again, disapproval of the earlier generations has always been the favorite sport of healthy youngsters, yet fathers and grandfathers do transmit to their children and grandchildren both genes and Oedipus complexes; some knowledge of the medieval components and irritants that went into the Renaissance cannot really do much harm.

Let us grant that a medieval economic historian may look at the Renaissance; but why should I be that one? My excuse is that I am a native Italian who has seen a good deal of that country: I was born in Genoa, of Tuscan parents living in Milan, and have taught Italian literature and art, besides history, to boys and girls as far south as Sardinia. Without claiming that we, Italians, own our Renaissance, I dare say that we stand closer to its heart than the northern "barbarians" who write about it. We do not regard it as a shock and a prodigy, but as the predictable outcome of the Italian Middle Ages. As a matter of fact, Italian universities provide no special chairs for Renaissance history—only for medieval and modern history, hazily divided by a date, 1492, which is more relevant to America than to Italy. That does not mean that the originality and splendor of the Renaissance go wholly unrecognized in its native country, but it does mean that there is no break in the Italian historical stream at the waning of the Middle Ages, and that the Renaissance might have flowed just as smoothly into Italian modern history if it had not been obstructed by King Charles VIII and Martin Luther.

We certainly do not claim that Italian natives should have a monopoly of interpretation. Without the foreign scholars who looked at the Italian Renaissance with almost the same amazement as the followers of Charles VIII and of Martin Luther—Jacob Burckhardt above all, and then a legion of friendly "barbarians" such as Hans Baron, Wallace Ferguson, Felix Gilbert, Myron Gilmore, Denys Hay, P. O. Kristeller, E. R. Labande, Raymond de Roover, to mention only a few senior statesmen who are still with us—the Italians might never have realized how original their Renaissance was. Half of its originality, however, was congenital: Italy was different from the rest of Europe in the Middle Ages as well.

This fact, too, is not unknown to non-Italian scholars; but the deep-rooted tradition of glossing over the Italian Middle Ages as a peripheral deviation from the norm rather than an outstanding anticipation of the European future has distorted or slowed down the study of the genetics of the Renaissance. Few are the people who, like Robert Reynolds and Frederic Lane, have stressed the modernity of the Italian Middle Ages without confusing it with the still greater modernity of the Renaissance.[1] More often, the latter has been bent backward to embrace the fourteenth century as a whole; to say nothing of certain textbooks where Dante, Giotto, even Marco Polo are exhibited as early specimens of the Renaissance man.

This, however, is going too far. Dante's allegorical journey among the dead, Giotto's suggestive play of shades without geometrical perspective, Polo's enchanting combination of mercantile and chivalresque lore are perfectly at home in the Italian Middle Ages. Of course the Italians of the thirteenth century resembled their descendants of the fifteenth more than their foreign contemporaries; but if we deny medieval credentials to all men who were city-centered, businesslike, literate, or individualistic, we might as well say that Italy never was medieval. This is, more or less, what Armando Sapori suggests in a provocative essay, but Sapori is, like me, an economic historian, and his argument is not designed to please art historians, especially if they are not Tuscans as he is.

Even the most perceptive "barbarians" find it difficult to keep Wotan's head off their manuscripts. To support his argument that a "mutational change" occurred in architecture between 1300 and 1600, Erwin Panofsky pointed out that Palladio's "Villa Rotonda," of the sixteenth century, is much more like the Roman Pantheon, of the second, than like Our Lady's Church at Trier, of the thirteenth.[2] This is certainly true, and no one has shown better than he did why the Italian Renaissance is the only "renaissance" that did not merely imitate certain traits of classic art, but made it live again. Trier, however, is in Germany, not in Italy. Had the three terms of comparison been chosen in one and the same Italian city, it would have been easy to perceive a consistent trend underlying the sharpest mutations of style. There is no clash in Florence between the early Romanesque façade of San Miniato, the Gothic belfry of Santa Maria del Fiore, and the Renaissance front of Santa Maria Novella; and if the wedding-cake Gothic cathedral of Milan does not fit snugly between the Roman balance of San Lorenzo or the Romanesque balance of Sant'Ambrogio and the Renaissance balance of Santa Maria delle Grazie, this is because the cathedral was built on a model supplied by foreign architects. In Italy, for better or for worse, the Roman stately tradition almost imperceptibly slid through Byzantine basilics and Lombard *opus romanense* into the ripe Italian Romanesque. Then, the Gothic style of the north belatedly passed the Alps, but it was not so much a great turn as a short detour before the conscious revival of Roman antiquity in the Renaissance. Italy's Gothic tempered its disembodied, vertiginous, sky-bound drive with reassuring features that anchored it to earth. Thin stone and glass yielded to meaty brickwork, or else alternate stripes of differently colored marbles debunked the vertical effort of the structure.

If some continuity may be observed even in the field where the contrast between Middle Ages and Renaissance was sharpest, it must have played a much more significant role where no "mutational change" took place between 1300 and 1600. In legal theory and practice, for instance, the only real turn occurred between 1050 and 1150, when Roman law got new wings at Bologna, the rediscovered Digest was triumphally carried away from Amalfi to Pisa, and a tract on jurisprudence denounced the "transalpine kings" who had "reopened the wound" of the invasions by imposing barbarian customs on the heirs of Rome.[3] Indeed, in some respects one might contend that the spirit of republican Rome was less alive in the Renaissance than in the heyday of the medieval communes, which were republics although they paid lip service to a universal empire, called "consuls" and "senators" their freely chosen rulers, and provided for their citizens a far better chance to lead the active civic life that so many Renaissance writers extolled while serving tyrants and oligarchies. Yet all this, and much else that could be said along the same line, must not becloud the substantial difference between the generations who admired ancient Rome but were proud of the material and moral achievements of the intervening centuries and the generations who rejected the entire medieval past to make a fresh start where Rome had left off. One might say, with some oversimplification, that the former found some faults with the present but looked forward to progress on earth and towards heaven, whereas the latter believed in cycles of growth and decay but felt that Rome had reached the summit of a cycle and aimed for the same peak.

Where is the watershed between the medieval and the Renaissance world views? The earliest acceptable divide, in my opinion, is the Black Death of 1346–48, which dealt a sudden blow to confidence in the future. Not long before, Giovanni Villani, the Florentine chronicler, after inspecting the Eternal City and reading her classic historians, concluded that "Florence, daughter and creature of Rome, was going up while Rome was going down." Respect for the memories, but a sober appraisal of contemporary Roman power—this is the attitude of a medieval Italian. Then, in 1347, Cola di Rienzo, a Roman notary, styled himself "tribune of the people and liberator of the Roman republic," and expected that the sheer magic of that name would command obedience. This is the first voice of the Renaissance. No doubt one may object that Cola's dream was shared by only a few people. But even later, when the dreamers multiplied, the ideals of the Renaissance, unlike those of the Middle Ages, were those of a minority.[4]

How many swallows do we have to see before stating that spring has come? No wonder opinions differ, especially when the later starts of the Renaissance outside Italy are taken into account. At a symposium held at the Metropolitan Museum some fifteen years ago, the moderator threw in the sponge: "It appeared quite impossible to reach any decision as to the historical limits of the period, or, indeed, to agree on a definition of the Renaissance itself." I was probably the youngest, obscurest, and hence most opinionated member of the panel. And I contributed greatly to the confusion, both by placing squarely in the Renaissance Giovanni Boccaccio, the older contemporary of "medieval" Chaucer, and by insisting that an economic historian sees no sharp divide at any point between the great plague of 1346–48 and the great inflation of the late sixteenth century.

I have mellowed in the course of years. It is pleasant to think of the Italian Renaissance as a lovely creature, whose youth, maturity, and old age should be defined within limits not exceeding too much the possible life span of a woman; to be generous, not much more than a hundred years. A beautiful lady should be entitled to a long youth, a somewhat shorter maturity, an undragging decline. Let her be born, like Botticelli's Venus, full grown in her prime; let her not waste away slowly, but be put to sleep before she becomes a sorry ruin. Through these contrivances, whose unorthodoxy I shall not deny, we can pare off the uncertain, transitional periods, come closer to the chronology of the retarded northern Renaissance, and assign to the three ages precise limits which have at least an uncontroversial political significance.

Youth may begin in 1453, when Constantinople fell to the Turks, or 1454, when that ominous event cowed the Italian states into forming an uneasy league. Maturity will break in forty years later, not promptly when America is discovered and Lorenzo il Magnifico dies (1492), but in 1494, when Charles VIII begins the series of foreign invasions and Pico della Mirandola passes away. The sack of Rome thirty-three years later by the soldiers of Emperor Charles V used to be entered in old-fashioned manuals as marking the death of the Italian Renaissance at the murderous hands of transalpine Protestants; this seems too much, but we may adopt that date, 1527, as the end of maturity and the beginning of old age. Besides, Machiavelli died in 1527. This leaves another thirty-two years before 1559, when the treaty of Cateau-Cambrésis freezes Italy under the political control of Spain, and religious control, of which many links have already been hammered down by the early meetings of the Council of Trent, finds one of its most effective tools in Paul IV's *Index of Forbidden Books*.

The three subdivisions, I believe, actually correspond to different climates. The prevalent mood of youth is confident expectation, that of maturity fluctuates between self-assurance and disenchantment, that of senescence tends to despondency. I hope to show that those three attitudes were in turn paramount during the three ages of the Italian Renaissance within the chronological boundaries just traced; more distinctly so in such fields as literature and politics, which are geared to emotions, but to some extent in abstract architecture and cold economics as well. Do I have to add that moods can never be unanimous? Generations overlap; each generation has its optimists and its pessimists; most men modify their attitudes as they grow older and the world around them changes. Oversimplification is the price of generalization; but the price will not be excessive if my sketchy triptych can catch a trace of the studied simplicity for which the Italian Renaissance strove.

Under cover of their studied simplicity, however, the best representatives of that culture entertained an omnivorous craving for knowledge and experience. A historian can hardly understand the "age of the well-rounded man" without a well-rounded approach; but who is well rounded enough? And who can encompass the universe of Leonardo da Vinci, but Leonardo himself? As I prepared my lectures for publication, it became more and more obvious to me that my way of using works of art and literature arbitrarily, as just another type of document, may seem outrageous to the specialists in the field; that my philosophy is much shallower and hazier than that of the average Renaissance philosopher (himself not a very deep or very clear thinker); [5] that my poaching in other specialists' preserves has led me to underplay economic and social history, the one field where I have specialized and written a few documented if controversial papers. My notes cite only an impressionistic selection of the works I have read, and what I have read is, of course, not enough. At the end of his essay on Machiavelli and the Renaissance, Federico Chabod, a man whom I loved and admired, placed a forty-seven-page bibliography. [6] I suppose the fields outside my bailiwick are adequately taken care of therein, but I find the economic and social aspects insufficiently covered. Still I doubt that Leonardo could have done as much as he did, had he read all the books listed by Chabod; and I am not Leonardo. Let my little triptych face critics as best it can.

ENTIONING the Italian Renaissance to a lusty layman is enough to bring a twinkle to his eye, as if one talked about a beautiful, talented movie star whose earnings are fabulous but whose private life is replete with scandal. That used to be the opinion of scholars as well, but recent research has led many of them to think that morality was less deplorable and economy less enviable than they look at first sight. We do not have to talk morals at once; let us first peep at the pocketbook of the Renaissance.[1]

Economic historians nowadays like to report on their subject with the reassuring, if sometimes deceiving, precision of statistical tables and diagrams. Unfortunately, the study of economic trends has lagged behind that of more glamorous aspects of the Renaissance. Although Italian archives do not lack quantitative data, such figures as are now available in print are too spotty to lend themselves to sound economic analysis. I can only offer an impressionistic picture, where judgments of value will bear the brunt of the argument, while numbers play a subsidiary role, not to prove a point but merely to illustrate it.[2] Numbers are not as photogenic as paintings and may be omitted here. Graphs are better looking, but only slightly. As a token of my respect for what the Young Turks of my discipline call "cliometrics," or economic measurement applied to history (and not without adding that in my opinion Clio is a muse, and her measurements ought to be 34–24–34) I shall exhibit the longest, most relevant, and least unreliable graph I have been able to construct.

This is a profile of the Genoese maritime trade from 1274 to 1530 as indicated by the amount of money a tax farmer paid in return for the privilege of collecting the main tax on the merchandise that entered or left the port. The solid line indicates the minimum value, in Genoese pounds of account, that the farmer expected to tax in order to break even. The dotted line adjusts the value to incorporate changes in the actual weight of gold corresponding to the increasing debasement of the Genoese pound of account between 1274 and 1530. Let me stress that the profile is not a precise representation of the ups and downs in Genoa's gross product. To say nothing of the fact that neither moneys

Graph I. Anticipated Maritime Trade of Genoa, 1274–1530
(1334 = 100)

of account nor weights of gold reflect possible changes in the purchasing power of precious metals, the difference between the expectations of the farmer and the tax actually collected must have varied; also, the all-time high of 1293 corresponds to the only case in which we have not the expectation but the total collection and hence may have to be slightly reduced. At any rate, maritime trade was not the only resource of Genoa, which also had land trade, banks, industries, a sizable territory, and substantial foreign investments. All this notwithstanding, the profile grossly agrees with all other information we have on economic trends in Genoa.[3] Scattered figures and nonquantitative data for other parts of Italy indicate that Genoa was fairly typical. Throughout Italy, though of course not without a number of local lags and exceptions, there was a great slump just before 1350, an alternation of partial recoveries and further decline in the second half of the Trecento, a low point some time before 1450, then stabilization on a lower level than before 1350, with a weak tendency to improvement, in the late Quattrocento.[4]

Much the same pattern emerges from whatever figures are available on population trends: a sharp contraction by 1350, then a seesaw on a lower level, with its bottom normally before 1450, then stabilization somewhere below the pre-1350 peak and a hint of recovery some time before the end of the Quattrocento. We have no long series of detailed and uniform data that can match that on the maritime trade of Genoa, but a sketchy demographic profile of Florence from 1280 to 1530, drawn according to the latest historical studies, may serve as an example.[5] Were it less sketchy, we would notice indentations corresponding to each visitation of the plague, which made its first, catastrophic appearance in 1346–48 and recurred periodically during the period covered by the graph, at intervals of from ten to fifteen years, with variable impacts. Between 1454 and 1494 the incidence of plague did not increase, but malaria, the product of old and new deforestation, overcropping, and inadequate water control, gained ground.[6] War was another agent of death; scarcely through battle casualties, for the mercenary armies of the period spilled money more lavishly than blood, but they scorched the earth and invited famine, which in turn bred disease. After 1454 the incidence of war became smaller; taxpayers felt little relief, for governments found other ways to spend, but the threat to harvests and traffic diminished.[7] There was no comeback for villages that had been abandoned and minor towns that were wither-

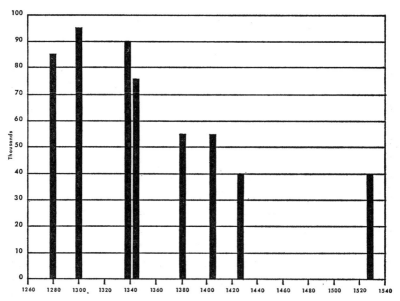

Graph II. Recorded Population of Florence, 1280–1530
(Clergymen and paupers are not included)

ing quietly, but agriculture rebounded in the more fertile regions, and the larger cities generally arrested or slowed down their decline. Of the four largest ones, two (Milan and Venice, but not Florence and Genoa) may have resumed their growth and attracted a trickle of immigrants, though nothing like the stream that used to flow in before 1350.[8]

In the long perspective of economic and demographic history, what we have called the youth of the Italian Renaissance looks more like an Indian summer than a new spring. In the shorter memory of people who had gone through the turmoil of the early Quattrocento, stabilization was a sufficient ground for prudent optimism, but certainly not for the buoyancy of the pre-1350 period. Most merchants, bankers, and artisans still pursued the trades to which they had been apprenticed in their early youth, but were on the lookout for new lines of business. They needed fresh foreign outlets to replace those which the collapse of the Italian colonies and privileges in the Levant, the internal crises of the Western monarchies, and, above all, the contraction of the aggregate purchasing power at home and abroad had made less receptive. They brought to their trade a close personal attention, and the highly rational techniques described in Benedetto Cotrugli's little book, *On Commerce and the Perfect Merchant,* which antedates Baldassar Castiglione's more famous work on the perfect courtier. These techniques defy summary description, but a few sentences of a more practical manual, that of Giovanni di Antonio da Uzzano, will be enough to indicate the self-confidence and sensitivity of the Italian businessman in the Quattrocento:

Never be eager to remit money where there is dearth, nor to withdraw it from where there is abundance. For wherever money is expensive, cash flows in from every place, money is withdrawn from banks, and therefore abundance is bound to come. But where there is great abundance, cash is drawn away, and money is bound to become tight. . . . I am not saying that when there is dearth you should not find yourself well supplied with money; but quite the reverse, you ought to have already made remittances there, so that you have money at good price where there is dearth. . . . And likewise in regard to merchandise . . . but do not buy commodities when they are dear . . . for you must consider that after dearth follows abundance.[9]

Whatever the circumstances, the businessman kept his chin up. He knew that "whereas a simple and plain receipt of a merchant is valid even without witnesses, the rulers and any other people are not believed without a notarial instrument and strong cautions." This and other realistic remarks add credibility to Cotrugli, whose farfetched quotations from Roman and Greek philosophers might otherwise bewilder a reader accustomed to modern economic statements. To prove that "the progress, the comfort, and the health of republics to a large extent proceed from merchants," he points out that trade promotes industry and agriculture, enables the poor to live, and enriches the public treasury. All this is true, but his enthusiastic picture, which would have described perfectly the economic growth of the twelfth and thirteenth centuries, leaves in the shade certain imbalances of the Quattrocento recovery.

The Italian economy of the Renaissance was less diversified than that of the Middle Ages. It rewarded prudence more than initiative, experience more than innovation, capital more than labor; it did not neglect entirely the most important bulky goods, but leaned very heavily on luxury trade and monetary speculations. Meanwhile, the demand for all commodities tended to lag, profits and interest rates were low or risky, and taxation was too high for comfort. Business still attracted fresh manpower and investments, but hardly enough to replace the old men who failed or withdrew. Some disenchanted businessmen buried their capital in real estate; others burned it up in conspicuous consumption; quite a number converted it into books and works of art. None of this was a new departure, for merchants had always bought land, luxury, and culture; but the emphasis and the motivation did change. Giovanni Rucellai, the second richest man in Florence, stated that he had become a patron of art because he got greater satisfaction from spending money than from gathering it. He was too proud to add that he had been losing money for many years, and that art had become a good investment, if only as the credit card of the elite.[10]

As a matter of fact, the society of the Italian Renaissance was no longer open and not yet closed. It could not be aristocratic in the same way as that of feudalism or of the Ancien Régime. The bourgeoisie had long before surpassed the income and destroyed the pride of the nobility; indeed, in many towns noblemen had been forced to renounce their titles and their way of life if they wanted to enjoy the full privileges of citizenship. Neither could it be a truly democratic society. The long depression had braked and finally stopped the checkered but relentless climb of the lower classes, which had brought economic and political opportunity virtually within everybody's reach. No doubt, opportunity did not die, and the upturn of the late Quattrocento restored some of its strength; but it was limited to a small number of people, and this opened a large gap between the rich and the poor, the superman and the underdog. The new elite was made up of different and ill-defined strains: those who had inherited wealth and prestige from ancestors who had acquired them while the going was good; those who had grabbed wealth and prestige by extraordinary ability, industry, and good luck in hard times; and those who had earned wealth and prestige by excelling in the arts, in literature, in learning, in some professional skill. The ideal Renaissance man, however, combined all requisites: he came from a good, old family, improved upon his status through his own efforts, and justified status by his own intellectual accomplishments.[11]

What accomplishments? The old and worn definition of the civilization of the Italian Renaissance as an age of individualism comes handy, not because there were many outstanding individuals (every age has its own) or because individuals were uninfluenced by their environment (this is hardly possible), but because an individual who wanted to be outstanding had to work hard at it. Long before the Renaissance, all aspects of education had made giant strides in the Italian cities that were to be its home. A considerable proportion of the urban population was literate, a large number was versed in accounting, commoners made public speeches or composed witty diaries, quite a few men dabbled in the arts and went to schools of higher education. Many citizens also mastered the skills of the nobility, from horsemanship and fencing to holding a fork and playing the lute. To this list, the educators of the early Renaissance had little to add except greater proficiency, but they told all men who would emerge above the vulgar crowd that they must display their ability in all fields at once. This was a great challenge for people who had leisure and talent (not necessarily genius), and it built up an in-group whose standards, drives, and emotions gradually lost contact with those of the mass. Well-rounded knowledge, cultural refinement, and aloofness also set the Renaissance gentleman apart from ordinary plutocrats and cutthroats, but made him something of a narcissist and a snob.[12]

It will seem flippant to append the last two terms to the moral portraits of the more towering figures. Surely Leonardo da Vinci, who called himself "omo sanza lettere" (unlettered man) and listed architecture, sculpture, and painting last in the long catalogue of practical skills he could place at the disposal of the duke of Milan if he was hired, was not a narcissist or a snob. But neither was he a regular Renaissance gentleman: he had come to town from the village where he had been born and raised, the illegitimate son of a peasant maid and a notary. Not so Leon Battista Alberti, the scion of an old and proud merchant family of Florence, who is often cited as the prototype of the universal man. He does not forget to extol the commercial achievements of his ancestors, and to praise the traditional virtues of the merchant, among which honesty, diligence, and *masserizia* (economy) are paramount. Yet he draws an invidious distinction between the nonprofit liberal arts and those "ugly and vile arts in which those old men who esteem wealth more than honor educate the young." Still more typical is the following piece of advice: "There are certain things a man must spend all his will, diligence, and study in doing well . . . : to ride, to dance, to walk in the street, and the like. This above all: he must tone down with painstaking care his gestures, expression, motions, and posture . . . so that nothing may seem to be done with conscious artifice. Let him who sees you believe that such grace is a natural gift." Taught in the best Renaissance schools and practised in the best circles, this manufactured spontaneity is not so much artificial as artistic; after all, the two words come from the same root. It expresses the ripe sophistication of urban residents, whose first preoccupation is to look at themselves in a mirror, no matter how urgent the business at hand. "Not without blame," Alberti continues, "may a civil man look hurried, as if driven by many things he has to do." [13]

Let us not stop at the surface. Composure and detachment are not merely the passport of the well-bred man: they impress their mark on Renaissance art and enable Renaissance thinkers to perceive the difference between politics and morality, banking and usury, ideal and reality, more clearly than had their medieval predecessors. Civility and urbanity imply much more than balance and good manners: they encompass all that makes city life exciting. The civilization of the Italian Renaissance was exquisitely urbane not only because it was urban—ever since the Etruscans, Italy's leadership had rested on cities —but because immigration from the country had nearly stopped for almost a century, and such *contadini* as still came to town during the late Quattrocento were expected to shed their rustic habits as quickly as they could. No longer a terminus of frontier trails or a bustling thoroughfare, the city was much like a theatre, where people shed their "muddy clothes" to don, like Machiavelli, "royal and courtly ones."

Nevertheless the fact that the city elite had lost immediate touch with the country made its members more eager to get some whiffs of uncontaminated suburban air, look at the landscape, and, while there, observe with sympathetic bewilderment the peasants, who might have the secret of honesty and happiness in their artless ways. Add that farming was not at all a bad investment while commerce and industry were barely picking up after the long depression; moreover, no snobbish (that is, nonnoble) society can be totally indifferent to the quasi-feudal prestige that seems to go together with the ownership of land. All this, as well as the influence of the agrarian and pastoral vein running through the classics, helps explain why such a large proportion of Italian literature in the late Quattrocento, though written almost exclusively by and for inveterate city dwellers, is concerned with country life. [14] To say nothing of Jacopo Sannazaro's *Arcadia,* which is no closer to real peasants than Marie Antoinette's toy village at Versailles, there are two little poems, *Nencia da Barberino* (probably by

Lorenzo il Magnifico) and *Beca da Dicomano* (by Luigi Pulci), which endeavor to depict rustic loves in rustic language. Still better, Angelo Poliziano's musical *rispetti* raise folk song to the dignity of high poetry. There is no reason to doubt the sincerity of this revived interest in the country; but it was an attitude more than a commitment, and it seems exaggerated to call it a rediscovery of Nature. The townsman did not swap his lute for the reed pipe, and if he retired to the country, he tried to reproduce in the gardenlike surroundings of his villa the studied simplicity of his city house.[15]

The renewed appeal of the world of chivalry in the late Quattrocento is not so easily explained. No doubt tournaments and cavalcades enabled the upper class to display sportsmanship and fancy dresses; noble titles and gestures improved the appearance of illegitimate princes and mercenary captains. For a bourgeois and Ciceronian elite, however, such feudal trappings were not so much an exercise in nostalgia as a pretense or a plaything. Still, you do not have to believe in Santa Claus to trim a Christmas tree. Whether in stylish garb or in rustic disguise, the knights of yore had lost none of their audience; they supplied an excellent pretext for the epic poems of an unepic age, Pulci's *Morgante* and Boiardo's *Orlando Innamorato*. Pulci's poem is more consistently tongue-in-cheek; whenever his Roland comes too close to emotion, a clownish joke reminds us that the author is unmoved. The real heroes—or should we say antiheroes?—are two rogues, giant Morgante and half-giant Margutte, both endowed with a gargantuan appetite and an almost disarming amorality. Margutte, especially, is a perfect scoundrel, but we cannot get angry at a man who dies of laughter and keeps laughing even in Hell. Then there is a learned devil, Astarotte, who predicts that men will find another inhabited world to the west of Gibraltar; we suspect that he heard from Paolo dal Pozzo Toscanelli, the cosmographer and friend of Pulci, the same theories that a few years later will spur Christopher Columbus on the way to the Indies. Boiardo's poem has still more characters, but few of them fully alive. While admiring the fantasy that contrived the innumerable plots interwoven in *Orlando Innamorato,* we miss the genius of Ariosto, who continued those plots in *Orlando Furioso*. It certainly was hard luck for Boiardo to be eclipsed by an unforeseen continuator; still we have to admit that his work falls between two stools. The poem is neither skeptical enough to discredit the chivalric ideals nor convinced enough to uphold them. Its style is too gentlemanly to attain Pulci's comic vigor, yet too rough to approach Ariosto's exquisite elegance.[16]

Hard though he might try, the Renaissance gentleman could no more feel at home in a castle than on a farm. The classic rhetoricians and moralists whom he read with increasing zeal told him that he could best display his manliness or "virtù" (from *vir,* man) by taking active part in the political life of his city. This is exactly what his closer ancestors, who read more Christian than pagan authors, had been doing ever since the communes gained their independence in the twelfth century. Unfortunately, the theory of civic participation came to maturity at the same time as practice became difficult. Political developments paralleled the economic ones: a long crisis ended in an uneasy standstill. At first, the economic slump hardened the resistance of smaller cities threatened by the expansion of their neighbors, and embittered the internal feuds in each city; but in the long run, only the wealthier cities and the richer people could maintain adequate mercenary armies and keep on fighting. Before the end of the fourteenth century, the lower classes had been almost everywhere defeated, and nearly all of the minor cities had been conquered or reduced to a marginal existence. At the center of the stage, ducal Milan and republican Florence were locked in a duel which gave the propagandists of the two sides an excellent opportunity for debating the advantages of "peace" under a *signore* or "liberty" under a larger but by no means all-embracing body of citizens. It matters little that the price of internal peace was unquestioning obedience to a lord who was forever engaged in foreign wars, or that the counterpart of liberty for the full citizens was restraint for the other inhabitants of the master city and subjection for the inhabitants of the other cities and villages under it. Even today, "peace-loving" and "democratic" are most ambiguous terms. The Milan-Florence duel became a five-cornered contest during the early Quattrocento, while republican Venice was making her own bid for supremacy and while both monarchic Naples and the Papal State were throwing on the scales their large but flabby bodies politic. Still there continued to be writers who exhorted all good men to prove their worth by participating actively in the political life.[17]

After 1454, however, these exhortations became totally unrealistic. The newly formed Italic League did not introduce perpetual peace, but limited the scope of wars. It fastened over the country a shifting balance of five great powers, whose mutual suspicions enabled the surviving small powers to live on, but whose common fear of revolution prevented any effort at modifying political organizations except in a more conservative and authoritarian direction. Three of the great powers—Milan, Naples, and the Papal State—had a long autocratic tradition. Despotism could be tempered by the rulers' inefficiency, fear, or good will; but the latter was a rare commodity, fear diminished as the sovereigns consolidated their power, and the Sforza dukes of Milan were fairly efficient. In Florence, physically the smallest of the great powers, the old rivalry of merchant oligarchic families had given way to the uncrowned monarchic rule of the wealthiest one; the republican name and institutions still persuaded Lorenzo de'Medici to speak softly, but he carried a big stick wrapped in gold. Only Venice among the five great powers was a true republic, where decisions were taken jointly by the restricted number of families who for centuries had monopolized the high offices; but political writers were barely beginning to realize that what formerly had seemed a narrow oligarchy was now, under the prevailing circumstances, the best formula to achieve a minimum of both peace and liberty. Proud Genoa, Venice's old rival, now alternated brief spells of republican turmoil with voluntary subjection to either France or Milan. There were a few smaller republics with a larger measure of popular government, but Siena, the most notable among them, led a most agitated life, thus confirming the widely accepted theory that rule by the rabble is the worst of all tyrannies. The majority of the small states were under autocratic *signori*: Savoy in Piedmont, Este in Ferrara, Gonzaga in Mantua, and so forth. Henceforth only an occasional, foolhardy worshipper of Brutus, such as Stefano Porcari in Rome and Gerolamo Olgiati in Milan, would take up arms for the ideal of civic virtue and be executed amidst the indifference of the rabble.[18]

To be active and thrive, an ambitious man who did not happen to be himself a prince had now to play whatever tune the prince wanted to hear. Even a *condottiere* was no longer a free agent: Jacopo Piccinino, the only mercenary captain after Francesco Sforza who tried to grab a state for himself, was eventually executed by the king of Naples. More wisely, Bartolomeo Colleoni accepted riches and honors as compensation for being eased out of active command of the Venetian troops. An accredited humanist might still try to sell flatteries to the highest bidder, as did Francesco Filelfo and Porcelio Pandoni, the author of a chronicle where Sforza and Piccinino are so consistently called Hannibal and Scipio that one wonders whether the clock of history has not run amuck. Only faithful service, however, would insure a rhetorician a steady administrative or diplomatic career. He might be less deeply committed than he sounded, but not necessarily insincere: "my prince, right or wrong" is not a more illogical saying than "my country, right or wrong," and there always are people who will not conceive that any government may ever be wrong. Francesco Patrizi, born in radical Siena but cooled by his career as a bishop, mustered excellent arguments in favor of both the republican and the monarchic government in two successive books which enjoyed the widest popularity.

If the late Quattrocento offered little opportunity for civic virtue and political dedication, were the prospects for Christian virtues and religious dedication more brilliant? Any answer hangs on debatable values and uncertain quantities. The Italian Renaissance had more than its share of saints, but sanctity is not the only form of virtue: virtue is not easily defined and not recorded in any census. Neither are there any statistics of vices, and even crimes go down in history only when they amount to works of art. Nobody will deny the artistic hand of the Italian Renaissance in this particular field, but one wonders whether our generation, which has witnessed genocide and stockpiles nuclear weapons, has any right to condemn the hand-picked murders and localized war atrocities of that pre-industrial age. Again, the elite supplied leaders to the ecclesiastic profession and went regularly to church; but it does not help to debate whether the ingrained cynicism and dissipation of some spokesmen made a mockery of their devotional practices, or whether the innermost, unshaken confidence of some others in prayers, confession, and repentance belied their ostentatious paganism of manners. Such contradictions may have been sharper in the Renaissance, but they are not peculiar to it. Ribaldry and piety, fear of the afterlife and agnosticism, have never been incompatible.[19]

The illustrious example of Aeneas Silvius Piccolomini, later Pope Pius II, stands out in our mind. He began his career as a most worldly humanist, but became more and more involved in the religious duties of the ecclesiastic habit he had donned as the best means for advancement. He continued nevertheless to make war, love, and Latin orations, but he died on the eve of sailing on a crusade. Every inch a Renaissance gentleman, Pius II was the only pontiff in history who not merely would have recruited others for the holy war, but intended to bear the cross himself. Surely that Sienese pope is no less typical of the late Quattrocento than Alexander VI Borgia, the Spaniard whom textbooks and novels play up as the epitome of Italian profligacy. Yet we must admit that it took an unusually well-rounded personality to combine Cicero and Christ as thoroughly as did Pius II. It was simpler to adopt one of two extreme solutions: either to give up the world of gentlemen entirely and live as an ascetic or a saint, or to play the pagan, worldly game with the great majority of both clergymen and laymen, while doing in private the minimum indispensable for the daily hygiene of the soul. It is not surprising that the second option fitted the way of life of the Renaissance elite better than the first.

A relaxed attitude, however, does not necessarily mean cynicism more than tolerance, disbelief more than reliance upon God's mercy. In the religious field, as in economic and political matters, we can speak of stabilization after a long crisis, although the timing was not exactly the same. In Italy the age of anxiety, heresy, and reform of the clergy had spent its impetus by the second half of the fourteenth century, when Boccaccio noted in the first story of the *Decameron* that "God's benevolence does not consider our mistakes but the purity of our faith. If we address Him through one of His enemies whom we believe to be His friend, He listens as if we had recourse to a true saint." In the Quattrocento, most people trusted that even the unworthiest clergyman had in his hands the indispensable tools to help laymen toward salvation, and few people feared that salvation might be endangered if the traditional and somewhat vulgar manifestations of cult were embellished with some pagan refinement. The growing interest in non-Christian philosophy was by no means a religious revolution, but above all a literary and artistic fad, in keeping with the aesthetic cult of classic authors. In less permissive times, the Catholic church had taken the Platonic strain of Augustine, then the Aristotelian strain of Aquinas in its stride. The new influx of Platonic doctrines through Marsilio Ficino and the artists who gathered around him, in what was improperly called the Florentine Academy, could not alarm the Church of the Renaissance. So long as beauty was praised as an earthly reflection of the infinite beauty of God, there was nothing wrong in searching for beauty; nor was Ficino's mystic pantheism entirely inconsistent with the Christian concepts of illumination and grace. It would take the intransigence of the northern Reformation to point out that Platonic Christianity tended to deflect man's interest from God's heaven to the God-filled nature of which man was the center, and made the Church almost peripheral to his soul.[20]

Important though Platonism was, we must not exaggerate its influence; the civilization of the Renaissance was not a work of philosophy but a work of art, as Jacob Burckhardt taught us. While Florence mused on Plato, Padua and Venice still favored Aristotle; yet the mood of the elite was scarcely different. When Aristotelian Ermolao Barbaro bragged that he acknowledged only Christ and literature, he was only half-joking. Christ was higher, but literature was supreme on earth. The Renaissance gentleman was losing the floating feeling of inferiority that had accompanied the first phase of humanism: he knew all the tricks of Latin and a growing amount of Greek, but he had recovered pride in his language. This was a rather sharp turn, and a healthy one. Over the centuries, ancient Rome has been for the Italians both a stimulus and an obsession: they can neither forget it nor reproduce it. The early humanists knew that no city-state in their time could match old Rome's military power, found the religious supremacy of Italian popes an insufficient substitute, and strove in vain to revive the civic virtues of their ancestors. They succeeded, however, in removing from Italy's Latin the incrustations of the barbarous centuries. Rome's language, in the words of Matteo Palmieri, "began to shine forth in its ancient purity, beauty, and majestic rhythm." Then they realized that its splendor had dulled that of Italian: hardly anything of poetical distinction appeared in the vulgar tongue in the early Quattrocento, and a contest for a poem that would match in Italian the beauty of Latin poetry (1441) ended without a winner. Vernacular prose fared somewhat better, but it had always played second fiddle to Latin except in fiction, and the short story, too, produced nothing of outstanding merit.

The late Quattrocento reestablished the balance: the younger poets had finally mastered the language of their forefathers enough to readopt that of their mothers as well. Only one of them, perhaps the greatest—Giovanni Pontano—accepted no compromise: he was a Neapolitan but would be every inch a Roman. He changed his Christian name to that of an emperor of the decadence, Iovianus, composed for his son enchanting Latin lullabies, got him a nurse learned enough to sing them, and in his vast literary production never condescended to the vulgar. There is a penalty for turning one's back to one's time. Both Catullus and Petrarch, each of whom wrote the language of his contemporaries, are still read widely, but only a few scholars are aware of the greatness of Pontano. Wisely, the other poets of the late Quattrocento made peace with their age. Some of them handled Latin as easily as did Pontano (Politian was at home even in Greek), but they entrusted their glory, and that of the Italian Renaissance, mainly to the vernacular. It is true that most of them were from Tuscany, the home of the purest Italian and the fatherland of Dante, Petrarch, and Boccaccio. One does not discard such a legacy lightheartedly.[21]

To go back to Palmieri, an intelligent Florentine, who lived astride the mid-Quattrocento and was far from insensitive to the spell of Dante: is it not strange that he found the refurbished Latin and the resurgent artistic proficiency of his time sufficient reasons to look forward to "a new age, full of hope and promise, which already rejoices in a greater array of gifted souls than the world has seen in the thousand preceding years"? Was he altogether blind to the many economic, military, political, moral problems of his day? Did he really think that the benefits of a purer Latin meant more, for the majority of the Italians, than the scourges of corruption, aggression, exploitation, and disease? Probably not: his memoirs, and his expression in Antonio Rossellino's bust, show him a keenly compassionate man; but his priorities were those of a society which regarded artistic and literary glory as the supreme earthly achievement. Is this really more strange than our reaching for the moon while so much is amiss on the earth? As Lorenzo il Magnifico put it in a letter composed by Politian for him, Achilles would be nobody without Homer, and Pisistratus, the wise prince of Athens, nobody if he had not preserved Homer's poem for mankind. The point may have been overstated, but Lorenzo's life proves that in this instance, at least, he was speaking frankly. He certainly hoped that his poems and his promotion of arts would insure him more enduring fame than his clever politics and unscrupulous finance. As a matter of fact, they did. At any rate, it was not within the power of a few individuals to turn the economic or political tide—and it may have seemed enough that things settled down in the late Quattrocento—but the battle of letters had been won. This prompted Benedetto Accolti to state that although the classics had set a sublime model, his contemporaries had so well learned their example that they were at long last ready to surpass it.[22]

This claim invites comparison with a well-known allegory that medieval scholars liked to quote: a Christian versed in the learning of the pagans was like a dwarf hoisted on the shoulders of a giant. The Renaissance scholar was both humbler and prouder than that. He was not sure that baptism alone placed him above his pagan masters—had

Hermes Trismegistus, Plato, Zoroaster, Averroës, the Cabbalists, not divined truths that are not soluble in holy water?—but he hoped that his own efforts might raise him to the same height as an ancient giant, and possibly higher. The most ambitious statement of this position is the *Oration* of twenty-year-old Giovanni Pico della Mirandola. That man is a microcosm, both central in the created universe and potentially closest to God, had been said not only by Ficino but also by many medieval writers. No one before Pico, however, had affirmed bluntly that every man is "the moulder and sculptor of himself" and can freely choose whether he will degrade himself to the level of brutes or lift himself up to that of angels and heavenly beings. To be sure, not everybody shared his belief in the individual power of self-improvement; Luigi Pulci, in his tongue-in-cheek description of cynical antiheroes, seems more inclined to stress the power of self-degradation. How actually free was free will in the face of God's foreknowledge? How strongly could man resist the influence of stars? How far could virtue, that is, manliness, prevail over adverse fortune? These very old debates were still unsolved. Certainly the road to perfection was not open to the rabble, but to a small number of outstanding men. But Pico was outstanding thanks to his prodigious learning, his noble birth, his inherited wealth, his celebrated handsomeness, all enhanced by the most desired asset of that age—youth! [23]

There is nothing unusual in praising youth, but the late Quattrocento went farther than usual in stressing extreme youth, with many of the features that are often associated with it: slenderness, fragility, natural grace, self-absorption, eager expectation—and, the only cloud in a clear spring sky, a dim foreboding of the short duration of happiness. Nowhere is this feeling more graphically expressed than in Lorenzo de' Medici's famous *Triumph of Bacchus and Arianna*—not a great poem, for its jumpy rhythm, plain vocabulary and conventional imagery reflect its origin as a musical song for carnival, but one as catchy as the great waltz of the *Merry Widow*. There is greater refinement, without loss of popular freshness, in Politian's garden and spring songs.

> Welcome to May and its banner of spray!
> Welcome to Spring, when love is the thing!
> Surrender, you belles, to amorous spells,
> don't say nay in May!

Here we find at its best that manufactured spontaneity which Alberti praised as the highest gentlemanly accomplishment: its elegance appeals to sophisticated minds, yet its simplicity speaks to the people. We are told, in fact, that country girls coming to Florence still sang Politian's poems two hundred years after his death; and we may count the ability of some poets and artists to reach for a broad audience as a partial compensation for the aloofness of the upper class.[24]

Actually Politian's poems are only one example of the mutual borrowings between popular and learned poetry, which can be traced as far back as written records go, and still occur today. His *rispetti* were preceded by the Venetian *strambotti* of Leonardo Giustiniani, a prominent statesman and humanist, who also wrote music for them. Here is a sample:

> The pope has granted fifteen years indulgence
> to any guy who'll be talking to you;
> a hundred fifty for touching your dresses
> and just as many for kissing are due. . . .

This impish, but not really irreverent theme also occurs in a few anonymous popular versions in Sicilian and in Tuscan. Indeed, even Petrarch's stylish sonnets have some parallels in dialectal verse. No doubt Italian audiences, in certain Renaissance towns and their vicinity, were peculiarly receptive to poetry; but this was mainly a legacy of the Middle Ages, which had spread literacy and art appreciation more widely in Italy than in the rest of Europe, and in Tuscany more than in the rest of Italy. Without minimizing this proficiency, we must keep in mind its limitations. By the early fourteenth century nearly all Florentines could read, but in 1450–59 almost one third of the witnesses to the extant notarial acts of Venice did not sign their names. Many villages hired school teachers at public expense, but in the early sixteenth century the notary of a village in the mountains near Lucca complained about children who "grow up without being watched, like wandering beasts." Above all, mere literacy is only the beginning of knowledge. Nevertheless, the topics of the Florentine poets, and of the painters who often used the same subjects and imagery, lent themselves to universal sharing better than the speculations of their common friends, the Florentine philosophers. It is not given to many to soar to the world of angels with Pico; but love comes easily, spring happens every year, and irretrievable youth always makes a wonderful sight.[25]

Three very young girls successively enchanted the Florentine people and inspired many writers and artists; their portraits would certainly have graced the cover of every magazine, if the newly discovered printing press had been producing such things at that time. The first was Albiera degli Albizzi, who became engaged, caught pneumonia at a grand garden party, and died at the age of fifteen in 1473, one year after the first edition of the *Divine Comedy* appeared in print. Forty-two poems, eulogies, and epitaphs, composed by famous men such as Politian and Ficino, paid tribute to the blond, black-eyed virgin whose untimely death had plunged the city in mourning. Not for long: two years later the same city reveled at a tournament in honor of blond, blue-eyed Simonetta Cattanei, whose banner, proclaiming her "la sans pareille," had been painted by Botticelli and was carried to prearranged victory by Giuliano de'Medici, Lorenzo's brother. Born of a Genoese family in well-named Portovenere (Venusport), peerless Simonetta had come to Florence to be the sixteen-year-old bride of Marco Vespucci, also sixteen, and the cousin of not yet famous Amerigo. She was twenty-three when consumption carried her away, to the despair of every Florentine, both famous and obscure. Then Giovanna degli Albizzi, Albiera's younger sister, became the star. She had received the excellent education that was far from uncommon among society girls: Venice-born Cassandra Fedele, for instance, wrote Italian, Latin, and Greek so beautifully that Politian decided she might even look pretty. Giovanna, however, was a real beauty, and her wedding to Lorenzo Tornabuoni was a memorable social event. She died in childbirth, at the age of twenty.

Glamor, in the late Quattrocento, called for physical frailty. One might kill the rose by picking it too early in the bud, and too many unplucked buds never grew into full flowers. Handsome men, too, were expected to be slim, and their life might be unnaturally abridged: Giuliano de'Medici was killed by conspirators; Lorenzo Tornabuoni was executed by Savonarola. One thinks of the impressive *Dance of Death,* an anonymous fresco in semirural Clusone (near Bergamo); it is approximately contemporary with Pico's *Oration,* and Pico himself died at thirty.[26]

Not death, however, but life and youth are the favorite themes of the painters, who often share with the writers both ideas and subject matter. We shall limit ourselves to very few examples: let us begin with Botticelli's most famous work, *The Birth of Venus.* Is this an allegory of Simonetta's birth in Portovenere? a pictorial rendering of Politian's images in the poem celebrating Simonetta's tournament?

These and other claims are both acceptable and debatable. More than Simonetta's only indisputable portrait, that of the Chantilly Museum, Sandro Botticelli's Venus resembles, of all people, today's movie star, Stefania Sandrelli, who was born a few miles farther south—a reminder that even the most idealized pictorial images usually have their prototype in the painter's own land. It is true that Stefania might find it inconvenient to have her left arm hinged in Venus' peculiar way. What does it matter? The essential fact is that in Botticelli's painting everything—women, men, shell, waves, Ligurian orange trees—have the manufactured spontaneity of Alberti and Politian. There are stronger and more intense works of art in the late Quattrocento, but no other is so slender and tender, so pretty and so pure. Even the mouth-blown breeze from the left, so helpful to show off Venus' hair, brings no clouds to the sky. It is but a fleeting harmony; in a moment, Venus will put on her cloak, the shower of roses will stop, and the suspended enchantment of nude youth will forever run away.[27]

One may question whether a masterpiece may stand as typical of an age: are not masterpieces by definition exceptional? Then let us go one notch down in quality and many miles away from Florence, which is the very center of Quattrocento Renaissance. Here is Gentile Bellini's procession in Venice's still unfinished San Marco square—a religious procession, to be sure, but who could tell it from a secular festivity? The scene is more pompous and less refined, for the Venetians were proud merchants, not semigods; but again we find elegance, harmony, joy of life, and a serene sky. A keen observer will note that the campanile has kindly moved to the left of where it actually is, so that we may catch a better glimpse of the Ducal Palace. Who would think, now, that there was a mistake in the planning of Piazza San Marco? We feel that the unsymmetrical campanile and palazzo felicitously break the uniform symmetry of arcades left and right; but in the late Quattrocento, Bellini wanted perfect harmony.

Our last example will be a Milanese miniature of moderate artistic importance; competence may reflect better than genius the fashion of the day. We see the second Sforza duke in the act of receiving a book of horoscopes from its author, Raffaele da Vimercate, who kneels down as obsequiously as if Milan had not tried to restore her free republic (unsuccessfully, it is true) shortly before. God is auspiciously at hand on the upper left, trying to center the ducal crown on the haughty head of Galeazzo Maria, whose posture shows how hard it is to manufacture spontaneity. Nature is there as an ornament; one can scarcely recognize the enclosed meadows and majestic trees that are the pride of Lombardy, so much are they trimmed and decorated. The fierce medieval coat of arms of the Sforza is incongruously supported by two weary *amorini,* who probably would rather join Politian's pretty girls and be crowned with the May flowers of the meadow. As for the horoscopes, they failed to warn the duke that he was going to be murdered shortly after; astrology, like econometrics, has its limitations.

. We cannot tell whether Galeazzo Maria liked the miniature: he was an elegant libertine, but dreamt of military glory, and had plans for an equestrian monument to his father, Francesco Sforza. No Renaissance prince had yet presumed to have a freestanding, full-size monument erected to his glory; the only postclassic example was Donatello's Gattamelata, of 1447, whose beautiful poise fits the ideal of civic virtue perfectly, although the hero is a *condottiere.* Then, in 1481, Andrea Verrocchio began work on a monument as dynamic as Donatello's is self-contained, that of Bartolomeo Colleoni. Completed long after Colleoni's death, the stunning sculpture does not really reflect the taste of that *condottiere,* which can be more easily reconciled with Amadeo's gaudy, if lovely, chapel and the gilt statue of Colleoni by a German sculptor in Bergamo. Francesco Sforza, both *condottiere* and prince, never had his monument. Leonardo da Vinci, to whom the work was eventually committed, made a gigantic model in clay, of which we have some idea from his preparatory sketches; but the model was broken by the French who overthrew the Sforza dukes, and Leonardo made other drawings for a less dramatic equestrian monument to Trivulzio, the Milanese *condottiere* at the service of the French. That, too, was never cast.[28]

One is tempted to conclude, in spite of two solitary masterpieces, that military heroism was uncongenial to the late Quattrocento. The sculptors of the period, like the painters, were more inclined to portray intelligent men, lovely girls, and smiling children. Four examples will take the place of a long comment. Pietro Mellini, who committed to Benedetto da Maiano the pulpit of Santa Croce, was not famous, but intelligence sparkles out from every wrinkle in his bust by Benedetto. We do not know for sure who was the delicate lady of Francesco Laurana's bust at the Louvre, but she could be a sister of Simonetta. Desiderio da Settignano's laughing child at the Vienna museum needs no arrows to win our love. To end with a religious subject: Luca della

Robbia's *Madonna delle Rose,* under the industrial shine of its poly-
chrome enameled terra cotta, presents in one package a slim lady, a
pudgy child, and impeccably decorative flowers.

It may be artificial to keep architecture apart from figurative art, as if
so many Renaissance artists had not practiced both at the same time.
Yet architecture's abstract components make it hard to link specific
buildings concretely with the passions and fashions of the age. Even
Piero della Francesca, that most architectural painter, lived in a dream
world of his own, unruffled by the emotions of the late Quattrocento
and hence closer to ours. Nonetheless, just as economic conditions
provided the Renaissance with a material foundation, so architecture
supplied a speculative ceiling—more effectively, perhaps, than the
somewhat hazy constructions of the philosophers. We must not look,
of course, for direct relations of cause and effect, but for some congen-
iality in the general mood. At the outset of the Renaissance, Brunelleschi and others had shortened the height and softened the angles of
buildings, in keeping with the classic and Romanesque tradition, but
they had preserved some of the Gothic slenderness. It seems not too
farfetched to say that this formula met the same ideal of beauty as did
the slender grace of Simonetta; for it was almost a dogma with
Renaissance architects that the human body should be the model of
individual buildings and whole city plans. Man's body, said Francesco
di Giorgio Martini, "is better organized than anything else." Studied
simplicity, the canon of Renaissance manners, also made headway in
architecture; for Gothic ornamentation had been choking in its own
exuberant tangle, and classic models suggested a more sober elegance.
Moreover, perspective was the thing, and pointed arches, in Filarete's
words, impeded vision. As for economic organization, we shall not
contend that it took Simonetta's body and Alberti's studied simplicity
as its conscious models; yet the economic conjuncture—a precarious
stabilization after a long downward trend—worked in the same direction. To face tighter and riskier markets, business had to become
slimmer, more flexible, more rational.

Architecture could change but slowly; remodeling a town calls for
greater effort than hanging new paintings on a wall. Only the elite had
the means to transform their houses, castles, and churches. Then, as
always, the wealthy often harbored conservative tastes. Though Filarete urged Francesco Sforza to abandon "this crude modern style" (that
is, Gothic), he was only allowed to smuggle some Renaissance touches

into old-fashioned structures. He found some comfort, like many modern urbanists, in drawing plans for a model town which was never built; a hierarchically conceived town, of course, for the Renaissance ideal was respectful of stabilized elites. Thus Alberti, who had opened the first wedges for the new classic style in Florence and Mantua, dreamt of a series of concentric, walled circles, where people of each class would live according to their status. A legion of great architects spread the new philosophy of building throughout the Italian cities and adapted it to villas, gardens, and fortresses. At first they obtained commissions for individual constructions, or at most for a prince's fantasy, such as Pius II's Pienza or Federigo da Montefeltro's Ducal Palace and grounds in Urbino. When Biagio Rossetti persuaded the duke of Ferrara to double the surface of his capital according to a Renaissance plan, between 1471 and 1505, the battle had almost been won.[29]

"To build," said Filarete, "is a voluptuous pleasure, like that of a man in love." There is something contagious in the narcissistic love of the late Quattrocento for its own art, its intelligence, its studied grace. Love makes every object in sight look brighter, but it is dangerously self-centered. While the Italian Renaissance leaders were picking flowers and setting traps for one another in their enchanting garden, they forgot the wild barbarians who were gathering all around the fences. It was a rude awakening when the fences caved in.

It would certainly be unwarranted to read a political prophecy in the Horatian invitation to "enjoy the day without trusting a later one" that forms the refrain of Lorenzo's *Triumph of Bacchus and Arianna*. Yet the lighthearted words of that lucky man happen to sound like a warning that carnival is almost over. They can serve as the closing note of the youthful Renaissance:

> Lovely youth, queen of all things,
> you forever run away!
> Let's be happy while we may:
> none can tell what next day brings.
>
> Here are Bacchus and his belle,
> fair, and bound with mutual spell:
> fickle time flies like a feather,
> but they spend it all together.
> Here are nymphs and other crowd
> merry making all aloud.

Let's be happy while we may:
none can tell what next day brings.

Those gay satyrs just beyond
of the nymphs are very fond,
in each cave and bushy patch
they made traps the nymphs to catch;
now that Bacchus has them tight,
they are jumping left and right.
Let's be happy while we may:
none can tell what next day brings.

Still, the nymphs are quite aware
they may fall into their snare:
when Love begs, who will say no
except people rough and low?
So they mix, no one is coy:
there is sport for girl and boy.
Let's be happy while we may:
none can tell what next day brings.

The big load that then will pass
is Silenus on an ass:
old, no doubt, but drunk and jolly,
full of fat, of flesh, of folly.
He can't walk, stand up or run,
yet he gets his share of fun.
Let's be happy while we may:
none can tell what next day brings.

After these, King Midas comes:
all he touches, gold becomes.
What's the point in having treasure,
for a man who gets no pleasure?
Gold tastes bitter, don't you think?
when you'd rather grab a drink.
Let's be happy while we may:
none can tell what next day brings.

Listen well to what I say:
do not wait until next day!
Happy members of this fold,
men and women, young and old,
pack your troubles, let them drop,
dance and laugh without a stop.

Let's be happy while we may:
none can tell what next day brings.

Girls and boys whose love is strong,
Love and Bacchus praise in song!
Each of you, sing, play and dance!
Fire your heart with sweet romance!
Oust all labor, oust all sorrow!
What must be, let be tomorrow.
Let's be happy while we may:
none can tell what next day brings.

Lovely youth, queen of all things,
you forever run away!

III Maturity 1494–1527

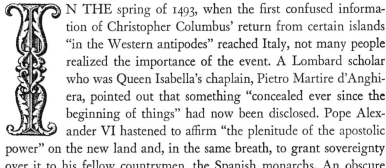N THE spring of 1493, when the first confused information of Christopher Columbus' return from certain islands "in the Western antipodes" reached Italy, not many people realized the importance of the event. A Lombard scholar who was Queen Isabella's chaplain, Pietro Martire d'Anghiera, pointed out that something "concealed ever since the beginning of things" had now been disclosed. Pope Alexander VI hastened to affirm "the plenitude of the apostolic power" on the new land and, in the same breath, to grant sovereignty over it to his fellow countrymen, the Spanish monarchs. An obscure Florentine rhymester quickly concocted in octaves an embroidered version of Columbus' first letter announcing the findings. That letter stirred up hopes that the naked inhabitants of the islands could easily be baptized (or, alternatively, enslaved), and that the meager samples of gold and spices brought back in the Spanish ships might be tokens of more to come. Still the excitement, in Italy even more than in Spain, fell short of Columbus' expectation. "Go West, young man" was not a popular slogan in a country where the best paths of adventure hitherto had led eastward, and the fact that the islands had not been noticed by the classics made them altogether less interesting for the elite. Besides, the long depression and uneasy recovery had weakened the daring of those very Italian merchants, who two hundred years earlier had rushed into the footsteps of Giovanni dal Pian del Carpine and Marco Polo; not, however, to a country of naked savages but to the splendors of China.[1]

In the following years a number of Genoese, who already had been busy developing and exploiting the Iberian peninsula and the earlier-discovered Madeira and Canary islands, transferred some capital, and in some cases moved personally to the "Indies." Yet when Columbus wrote nostalgically to the Banco San Giorgio, Genoa's greatest financial organization, that he had left his heart in Genoa and was planning to give her one tenth of his income, the bank put off a reply so long that Columbus never got the letter and his fellow citizens never received the money. Perhaps the administrators could not forget that the Admiral of the Ocean had once been a poor weaver, worried by his father's unpaid debts. Of course, not all the Italian seamen who played paramount roles in the great voyages were of such humble origin, nor were they all so ill-rewarded as Columbus himself or as Giovanni Verrazzano, who mysteriously vanished oversea and, according to improbable rumors, was either hanged as a pirate or eaten by cannibals. Simonetta's cousin, Vespucci, belonged to the elite of merchants and humanists, and gave his name to America. Sebastian Cabot became the governor of England's aristocratic Merchant Adventurers company. But no Italian had received a commission from an Italian government, and none was in a position to stake a claim for his native country in the new world.[2]

It is often asserted that Italy had no chance anyway: only an Atlantic nation was fit for transatlantic navigation; only a great monarchy was adequate for empire building. But this is an ex post facto rationalization. Long before 1492, the Atlantic had become like home waters for Italian ships, and more men and capital had been sent to the Italian colonies in the Levant than would later be needed for the conquest of Mexico and Peru. The duke of Milan could have patronized Columbus as easily as Leonardo; the Medici bank could have lent money to Florentine explorers more profitably than to foreign monarchs; Venice could have captured and held Cuba more securely than Cyprus. They did not, and the Italian Renaissance missed one of its greatest opportunities: not so much economic advantages or imperial gains, which seldom endure, as the chance to entrust the future of Italy's language and culture not only to a small European territory but also to an entire new continent. Yet who would have thought that such an expansion was needed, when all of Europe paid tribute to the grandeur of Rome and the talent of the Italian poets, artists, scholars, businessmen, and social leaders? Was Italy not glorious enough?

One year after Columbus' return, however, tragedy struck.[3] With the encouragement of the clever ruler of Milan, Lodovico il Moro, who felt threatened by the king of Naples, the dreamy king of France, Charles VIII, pressed his dynastic claims to the Neapolitan crown. His large army included French feudal cavalry, Swiss mercenary infantry, Scottish bowmen, and Europe's strongest artillery. Contrary to Italian military etiquette, Charles not only scorched the earth but also killed whoever resisted. This helped him to march through the peninsula to the Neapolitan border almost without a fight; the unpopularity of the king of Naples did the rest. Charles conquered the coveted kingdom in a few days. Isabella d'Este, marchioness of Mantua and sister-in-law of the Milanese duke, commented self-righteously that "all powers in the world should learn that one ought to rely more on the hearts of one's subjects that on fortresses, treasuries, and soldiers." Her remark would have fitted equally well the duke Lodovico il Moro, if his subjects had been then put to the test.[4] More compassionately, Matteo Maria Boiardo interrupted *Orlando Innamorato,* the chivalric epic of which he had composed no less than sixty-nine cantos for his own pleasure and that of the court of Ferrara, with the following octave:

> While I am talking, O Redeemer Lord,
> all of Italy is swept by the strong race
> of these French soldiers, who with fire and sword
> came to destroy I do not know what place.
> Hence I must leave unpluck'd the mournful chord
> of Fiordespina's love burning apace.
> Another time, if peaceful days prevail,
> you shall be told the story in full detail.

Boiardo died too promptly to see the turning of the tide and tell the rest of his story. It took only a few months for the Neapolitans to find the greed and insolence of their new master still more unbearable than the tyranny of the old one, and even the duke of Milan began to suspect that he had been less clever than he thought. There had been a shadowy Italian League, formed in 1455 and successively joined by all states from the Alps to Sicily, ostensibly "for the peace and quiet of Italy and the defense of the holy Christian faith" against the Turks. It had dissolved long before without hurting a single Turk, but the idea was still in the air and could be revived. Early in 1495, the major surviving states and some of the smaller began to gather an army against Charles VIII, who hurried back toward France. Met in northern Italy, near Fornovo, by the incomplete confederate forces (mostly

Venetian, with a disheartened Milanese contingent and a brave handful of Mantuans), Charles lost some face and all his baggage, but made good his retreat. Both sides called the bloody encounter a victory, but Lodovico il Moro promptly let down the Venetians and pledged again his help to the French king, should the latter make another try for Naples. Not Charles, who died three years later, but Louis XII, his successor, crossed the Alps again in 1499; and his first victim was the duke of Milan. The revengeful Venetians joined the French in the kill; the Italic League was gone beyond recall.

We must not leave the years which so unauspiciously ushered in the maturity of the Italian Renaissance without mentioning some accompanying calamities. As the followers of Charles VIII displayed their interest in willing and unwilling Neapolitan women, a hitherto unknown disease spoiled their pleasure. The French called it "le mal napolitain," the Italians "il mal francese"; but there is substantial if not indisputable evidence that it was one of America's first exports to Europe, which reciprocated by exporting smallpox to America. Its first impact was terrible on people who had no previous exposure and who, moreover, were just emerging from one of the worst periodical outbursts of plague. It was still a major scourge in 1521, when the nonchalant aestheticism of the Renaissance conjured up for it an elegant name—syphilis, after Syphilus the shepherd who catches the disease in a Latin poem devoted to it by Girolamo Fracastoro. A distinguished physician, astronomer-astrologer, literary critic, poet, and playwright, Fracastoro even managed to slip into his clinical verse some passionate allusions to the greatness of the ancient Romans and contemporary Italians. More relevantly, in a later book he maintained that infections are transmitted by self-multiplicating small bodies carried by ill people—which is not far from modern theories of contagion, especially if we consider that Fracastoro had no microscope.[5]

Yet the intellectual sharpness and refinement of the mature Renaissance were no bar to crude intolerance and superstition. Italy's traditional skepticism had always acted as a check against the worst excesses but was now beginning to yield, especially in the borderlands exposed to foreign influence. As early as 1475 the blessed friar Bernardino of Feltre prophesied in Trent, Italy's northernmost city and the southernmost imperial possession, that the Jews were about to commit a horrible crime. Obligingly, on Easter day, the body of a murdered child was found in a gutter: the German bishop of Trent charged the Jews with ritual homicide, and not even the pope could prevent the execution of thirteen of them, the expulsion of the others, and, later, the beatification of the child. Bernardino profited from this to stir up mobs against the Jews wherever he had a chance. Then, in 1492, the Spanish governors of Sicily enforced in the island Ferdinand and Isabella's decree of expulsion of all Jews. Henceforth trumped-up charges, violence, extortions, and expulsions occurred at many other places; but there was no consistent pattern of persecution. Many charitable souls tried to help the Jews (including refugees from Spain); many enlightened people appreciated their talents in medicine, the dance, and other professions; many princes found them irreplaceable as financial advisers, bankers, and merchants. The story of Daniel Norsa, a banker in Mantua, is an example of their precarious, yet not desperate position. In 1495 he had bought a house and obtained from the bishop, at a price, permission to remove from its wall a sacred image. He was nonetheless accused of sacrilege. The marquis of Mantua, just back from the battle of Fornovo where he commanded the Italian troops, confiscated the house and sentenced Norsa to pay for a painting by Andrea Mantegna in honor of the Virgin, who had granted what was called a victory. But he allowed no one to harm the banker; and Mantegna found it amusing to give one of the saints who surrounded Our Lady the features of Daniel Norsa. The joke may have been in poor taste, but it was a joke, not a tragedy. The bigots had their revenge in an anonymous, mediocre caricature of Daniel wearing the Jewish badge; the Norsa family continued to produce affluent bankers, one of whom was ennobled by the duke of Ferrara fifty years later.[6]

Black magic, on the other hand, suddenly stopped being a mere joking matter for sophisticated people and a rather harmless superstition for the plain folk. In 1484, for the first time, a bull of Innocent VIII gave official recognition to tales of successful sorcery in Germany, and thus opened the way for persecution in Italy as well. The following year, we are told, a first contingent of forty-one witches were burned at Como, and during the sixteenth century other fires were lit all along the Italian Alps. Nevertheless, the sorcery psychosis never spread from that northern periphery to the core of Italy. Witches still provided comic relief in a few poems and plays, and folklore provided a useful occupation for only one of them—the broom-riding "Befana" —who still today takes over from Santa Claus the task of placing charcoal in the stockings of naughty Italian children. As for black magic, it went on unmolested in the twilight of what has been called the Counter-Renaissance, the world of the rustic and the humble, who were out of reach not only of humanism but of the loftier aspect of Christianity.[7] Between Counter-Renaissance and Renaissance, the preaching of Girolamo Savonarola built temporarily a fiery bridge. Not unlike Bernardino da Feltre, Savonarola used his rugged eloquence and prophecy to arouse the fundamental religious emotions that never die. But he had a higher mind, a nobler heart, a better education; for a while he swayed not only uncultured proletarians, but some of the greatest artists and soundest bourgeois in Florence. He had forecast the invasion of Charles VIII, which he welcomed as the overdue punishment for the sins of Italy and a prelude to the imminent regeneration of the Church. The Florentines revolted against the weak son of Lorenzo il Magnifico, who surrendered to Charles their fortresses and money without a fight; still they were no match for the French might and knew it. The friar offered them not an impossible revenge, but self-mortification with a view to heaven. He persuaded them to set up a republic based on morality, a polity that tried to combine the aristocratic steering of Venice with the democratic impetus of pre-Medici Florence. The normally lukewarm Florentines were stirred up by Savonarola's continuous thundering against his enemies inside and abroad, including Pope Alexander VI, who first tried to ignore him, then excommunicated him. Twice, in 1497 and 1498, the bright fire of the "vanities" collected for burning in the Piazza della Signoria—fancy masks and dresses, playing dice, musical instruments, "immoral" books and paintings—proved that, even in Florence, Lent could prevail over Carnival. Yet all that fervor could hardly endure without further supernatural tokens or, at least, a measure of material success. Savonarola failed to recapture for the Florentines their lost territory and dodged a challenge to prove his mandate by the ordeal of fire. All his enemies fell on him; on May 23, 1498, the prophet and two of his followers were hanged, then burned, and their ashes were thrown into the river. The Florentines relaxed.[8]

The following year, as we have seen, Louis XII of France invaded Italy. The contest among "barbarians" for direct domination over some parts of the country and supremacy over the others started for good. For thirty years French, Spanish, Swiss, and German armies clashed on Italian battlefields, with many dramatic reversals of fortune. By 1527, the terminal date we have chosen for the "age of maturity," the Swiss had withdrawn with a minor part of the spoils, but the French still contested the evident superiority of the Spanish and German forces combined under Charles V. All the foreign contenders had consumed in the struggle a good deal of manpower and money that they might otherwise have used for the development of their own countries. The Italian states, of course, had lost much more: their independence, or their right to choose their rulers and policies, or at least their prestige and prosperity. War itself had changed nature and scope: the "battle of giants" at Marignano (1515) dwarfed that of Fornovo, and was, in turn, eclipsed by that of Pavia (1525); the expenditure of lives and money steadily increased with the number of combatants, the size of artillery and smaller firearms, and the ferocity of engagements. The Italians still played a fighting role in almost every encounter; but though in 1515 the intervention of the Venetian cavalry tipped the scales in favor of the French, and in 1524–25 the resistance of the besieged citizens of Pavia made it possible for the troops of Charles V to crush the French, it was always the Italian civilians who bore the brunt of the savagery of foreign armies. By 1527 there was hardly a part of the country that had escaped repeated plundering and physical violence. War also added impetus to the old scourges of high taxation, severe famines, and periodical returns of the plague. In 1529 two English envoys sent to their king the following report from what used to be the richest part of Italy, Lombardy between Vercelli and Pavia:

The moost goodly contree for corne and vynes that may be seen, is so desolate, in all that weye we sawe [not] oon man or woman laborers in the fylde, nor yett creatour stering, but in great villaiges five or six myserable personnes. . . . In this mydde waye is a town . . . all destroyed and in maner desolate. . . . [In Pavia] the chyldryn kryeng abowt the strates for bred, and ye dying for hungre. . . . There is no hope many yeres that Italya shal be any thing well restored, for wante of people.[9]

We do not have to go over the details in the various regions, but we can hardly dodge the much debated question of responsibilities for the disaster. If history were concerned with justice, the discussion might center on the wrongs of the aggressors; it is not, and hence we must look at the mistakes of the victims. There is no denying that the expedition of Charles VIII had demonstrated, on the one hand, that no single Italian state could stop a strong foreign army, but, on the other hand, that a confederation of Italian states could turn it back, whether or not it won a battle. Why did the Italian states not take the lesson to heart?

The basic, though not the only, reason is that the Italian princes and republics mistrusted one another as much as they disliked all outsiders to Italy. This is what Philippe de Commynes, the French historian and courtier, noted when accompanying Charles VIII; this is what emerges from the dispatches of the Italian ambassadors at one another's courts, whose numbers, industry, and intelligence could have wrought wonders if their task had been to foster harmony instead of spying on the anticipated evil intentions of each neighbor and hiding the crooked schemes of their own governments. All this is not unusual. Good will has never been the best part of diplomacy, sibling rivalry is the usual lining of cultural brotherhood, and hardly any modern democracy is innocent of having helped a dictator against fellow democracies. During the Renaissance no alliance could be more dangerous and objectionable than one with the Turks, but despair eventually drove the French to ask their help against Charles V. Without going that far, the Italian states had been far from united in this respect before 1494. Because Venice was the strongest and most feared among them, she was left practically alone to fight the Turks in the Levant from 1463 to 1479, though Pius II had asked for a crusade. Immediately after, the Turks landed in southern Italy and stormed Otranto with great bloodshed. It looked like the first move of an invasion by that very Mohammed II who had begun his reign by seizing Constantinople and might wish to end it by conquering Rome; yet nobody helped the king of Naples, Otranto's ruler, who was saved only by Mohammed's death. If before 1494 the Italians did not form a common front against the dreaded Infidels, why would they form it after 1494 against Christian foreigners? [10]

Indeed, Venice was the only Italian state rich and strong enough to hold out against any European power or coalition that did not include Turkey, and proved it in 1508–11. The largest alliance ever assembled during the Renaissance attacked her: it included France, Spain, the Empire, Hungary, and a number of Italian states led by the pope. Naturally, her armies were defeated and part of her territory was overrun; but defeats and invasion did not doom Venice, because unlike the other governments she had won the affection of most of her citizens and subjects, including even the peasants in the open country. Therefore she could wait for the inevitable dissolution of the league,

Upper left: Early Romanesque façade, San Miniato. *Upper right:* Gothic bell tower, Santa Maria del Fiore. *Center:* Renaissance façade, Santa Maria Novella.

Above: Portrait of Simonetta Cattanei Vespucci, ascribed to Piero di Cosimo (Musée Condé, Chantilly, France). *Right:* Portrait of Giovanna Albizzi Tornabuoni, by Domenico Ghirlandaio (detail of fresco in Santa Maria Novella, Florence).

Anonymous fresco, Chapel of the Disciplini Friars, Clusone near Bergamo.

Upper: Detail of *Procession in Venice,* by Gentile Bellini (Galleria dell'Accademia, Venice). *Lower:* The Piazza as it really is.

Galeazzo Maria Sforza receiving a book of horoscopes from its author (miniature in Biblioteca Trivulziana, Milan)

Upper: Probable portrait of Daniel Norsa (detail of *Madonna della Vittoria,* by Andreas Mantegna, in the Louvre, Paris). *Lower:* Caricature of Daniel Norsa (detail of anonymous painting in Sant'Andrea, Mantua).

Bust of Pietro Mellini, by Benedetto da Maiano (Museo del Bargello, Florence)

Bust of unknown lady, by Francesco Laurana (Louvre, Paris)

Bust of a child, by Desiderio da Settignano (Kunsthistorische Museum, Vienna)

The so-called *Madonna Benois,* an early painting by Leonardo da Vinci (Leningrad, Hermitage)

The so-called *Antiope* (Venus?), by Correggio (Louvre, Paris)

The Tempest, by Giorgione (Galleria dell'Accademia, Venice)

Above and right: Details of fresco by Moretto da Brescia (Palazzo Salvadego-Martinengo, Brescia)

Upper: Early Renaissance dome of Santa Maria Novella, Florence, by Brunelleschi. *Lower:* Late Renaissance dome of St. Peter's, Rome, wooden model by Michelangelo.

Upper: Head of David, by Michelangelo (Galleria dell'Accademia, Florence).
Lower: Head of Giuliano de'Medici, by Michelangelo (Cappelle Medicee, Florence).

The Pietà at St. Peter's, Rome

The Pietà at Santa Maria del Fiore, Florence

City gate at Verona, by Sanmicheli (detail)

Palazzo Grimani, Venice.

The so-called *Woman at the Mirror* (painted about 1515?—Louvre, Paris)

The so-called *D'Avalos Allegory* (painted about 1532?—Louvre, Paris)

The so-called *Venus Blindfolding Cupid* (painted about 1565?—Galleria Borghese, Rome)

whose members had conflicting ambitions and could afford disunion since they were not fighting on their own soil. This was perhaps the finest hour of the Most Serene Republic, but it taught her prudence. Henceforth, Venice strove to recover most of the land she had lost but abandoned whatever ambition of territorial expansion or leadership in Italy she might have. She was no longer feared as the paramount threat to the independence of other Italian states, but she did not yet appeal to them as the acceptable bulwark against the worse menace of foreign conquest. When Machiavelli wrote *The Prince* and invoked somebody like Caesar Borgia who might seize control over Italy and free it from the "stinking barbarian domination," he made no mention of the Venetian republic as a more suitable leader. For at heart Machiavelli may have been a stanch republican, but he still remained a Florentine hater of Venice; and though he exalted the unity of ancient Italy under the Romans and the Goths, he was no more impatient to see complete unification at once than most believers are to enjoy at once the eternal bliss of Paradise.[11]

The next in line for leadership was the pope. There were popes of all kinds: energetic as Julius II, lackadaisical as Leo X, wavering as Clement VII. Their usual line was trying to expel from Italy one of the "barbarians" with the assistance of another. They were much weaker and, in their own state, less popular than Venice; but the sanctity of their office gave them a measure of inviolability, which enabled them at moderate risk to switch alliances in a perpetual hunt for petty territorial gains. That some of the gains usually stuck to the fingers of a pope's nephew, or that political ambitions often took precedence over religious interests, did not seem too objectionable to most Italians; it was obvious that popes needed land to preserve their independence, and nephews to preserve their land. A growing number of people, however, agreed with Machiavelli that Italy could expect no help from the popes: they were too weak to unify it under their guidance, too strong to submit to anyone else who might unify it, too fidgety to quit inviting foreign intruders in the hope of using them as protectors. Nor was there any other Italian prince capable of learning the lesson of 1494 and "preparing his body to endure discomfort and his mind to be unafraid of danger." They all still "believed . . . that it was enough for a prince to think of a clever reply, write a well-turned letter . . . , contrive a fraud, wrap himself in gold and gems . . . , display towards the subjects greed and pride." Thus, again, Machiavelli, whose indignation, however, did not prevent him from prescribing cleverness, fraud, and greed to a prince who would keep afloat in the world where he lived.[12]

Under the strain of invasions, the artful humanistic ideal of civic virtue was disintegrating into its discordant elements. No doubt a prince ought to be both lovable and literate, but these moral virtues would be of no avail without the efficient virtues which both Pico and Machiavelli would ascribe not to the angelic but to the beastly drive of the self-moulder man. A prince "must be a fox to recognize traps, and a lion to frighten wolves." We need not insist on the foxy talents of the ruling classes of the mature Renaissance; they have been, if anything, overstressed, and it is far from sure that the Italians were really better at that game than their transalpine competitors. It is more questionable whether the Italian lions had adequate teeth. As early as 1503, during a contest between French and Spaniards for the possession of the kingdom of Naples, thirteen Italian knights at the service of Spain challenged thirteen French knights who had charged all Italians with cowardice and treachery; the Italians won the encounter, but in the end Naples lost its independence to Spain. Why were there not enough Italian princes capable of rallying the brave and talented individuals then serving under "barbarian" flags? Why were there not enough Italian fighters capable of crushing the "barbarians," as their Roman ancestors had done?

These painful questions, long a stock argument of literature, were raised with fresh timeliness in a few sonnets by Pietro Bembo, Luigi Alamanni, Giovanni Guidiccioni, Francesco Maria Molza, and others; but poets did not have to supply political answers. Machiavelli claimed that only "the weakness of their leaders" wasted the superior strength, dexterity, and intelligence displayed by the Italians in duels and individual encounters. As a remedy, he advocated armies of citizens, who would fight for their country and not for the highest payer. At long last the Florentine republic, of which he was the secretary, made a try at it; but the improvised militia was beaten by the professional troops of the enemy. Not even Venice, backed as she was by virtually all of her people, from gentlemen to peasants, could have won land battles without the specialized skill of mercenaries. On the other hand, mercenaries alone could not be expected to display the blind, stubborn, almost senseless courage that sometimes enables people fighting for their fatherland to triumph over desperate odds. "Fatherland," how ever, for most Italians was a petty state, ruled by an unlovable lord, a selfish oligarchy, or a somewhat larger group torn by internal dissensions—almost in every instance, a polity where a wide gulf separated the masses from the elite. If someone like Joan of Arc had arisen in Italy a hundred years after her appearance in France, she would have found no king for her cause: the only king on whose name all Italians might have agreed was Julius Caesar. Perhaps Caesar Borgia thought of it when he adopted the slogan "Either Caesar or nothing" at the start of his sinister, short-lived career.

Throughout Europe in the early sixteenth century, the national idea was mainly a literary and artistic image; in Italy, it was a retroactive dream. What could the literary and artistic leaders of the Renaissance do to defend the idea in the midst of the storm? Unlike medieval art, which was politically and religiously committed, Renaissance art was initially bent toward self-centered aesthetic harmony; it could not suddenly change its course without falling short of its climax. There were great praisers of beauty, but no Jeremiahs and no Goyas among the Italian masters of the early Cinquecento. Most of them had been born before the invasions and apparently still followed the formula of Leon Battista Alberti: a civil man may be grieved but must not let his grief interfere with his composure. That does not mean, obviously, that the tragic events of the early sixteenth century left no trace, or that the general mood of the mature Renaissance was as prevalently eager and serene as that of the earlier period. Even under the best circumstances, maturity can hardly recapture the blissful expectations of youth; but its pleasures are fuller, and its sorrows may be sublimated in the contemplation of an ideal that has been or can be attained. This occurs even with the most concerned writers. Machiavelli's *Mandrake* is at bottom a bitter play, but it has more zest and lust than anything written after the *Decameron*. His *Discourses,* his *Florentine History,* even the closing pages of *The Prince* surround the present gloom with the splendor of a glorious past and the hope of a triumphant future.

Not a deep thinker or a powerful writer, but a surprisingly decent man amid foxes and lions, Baldassar Castiglione sees no evil, hears no evil, and speaks no evil in his description of the ideal courtier. The ideal was not outright impossible, but too good to be true. Reality had provided Castiglione with a perfect ivory tower, a court where he had lived in his youth: the Ducal Palace of Urbino, a jewel of the youthful Renaissance, tucked away in the mountains and benevolently governed by an ailing duke and his warmhearted dame, who lived on inherited income and not on taxation. All the literary and military stars whom he imagines gathered in the palace to discuss the virtues of a perfect courtier, and of a lady worthy of him, are real people whom Castiglione actually met, and they might have expressed the opinions he ascribes to them. Yet the paragon that emerges from the combination of the best suggestions of each participant—a man who not only fulfills all of Alberti's canons of unaffected charm but also is unaware that he is unaffected—is not of this world. He reminds one of the flawless image a Greek painter was said to have composed by combining the best features of the five loveliest girls in his town. Today we would probably miss the imperfections that can make a girl more desirable, but classic Greece and the Italian Renaissance felt otherwise. Even as Gentile Bellini had eliminated irregularity from Piazza San Marco, so Castiglione amended the panorama of Urbino: Mount Catria, the highest peak, is not visible from the windows of the room where his imaginary symposium is held, but Castiglione moved it, so that it could be admired in the golden light of dawn. He hardly mentions economic and political problems: one of his personages hints that the Italian emphasis on literary achievements may have led to the French superiority on the battlefield, but quickly adds that "it is best to leave unsaid what cannot be recalled without grief." The book is, therefore, not so much idealistic as irrelevant; but it strikes a very responsive chord, the almost universal desire to belong to a better class of people. During three centuries at least, it continued to be read, translated, and accepted throughout Europe as the last word in exquisite breeding.[13]

Ludovico Ariosto is another sterling character and daydreamer, but his dreams have a higher and broader range than Castiglione's. It matters little that most of the personages and plots of *Orlando Furioso* are borrowed from Boiardo and earlier writers: the Renaissance, as most other ages before the nineteenth century, did not look for that kind of originality so long as the form was new and true to itself. Ariosto is probably the only writer who fulfills the ideal of unaffected grace which Alberti and Castiglione prescribed to others. He feels deeply, but does not seem to care; he moves fast, but does not look hurried. As he lets loose his imagination, he seems to forget the trials of the Christian world, of his country, of his own career at the service of two ill-mannered and heartless members of the ducal house of Este-Ferrara, Cardinal Ippolito and Duke Alfonso. Yet the wakeful half of his personality keeps emerging in gentle allusions to human suffering and foibles, or in unexpected sallies of self-deprecating humor. Only a couple of times does he let emotion force his hand: in an invective against Italy's folly, which echoes Dante, and in an original outburst against firearms, which have destroyed chivalry, and at present are making havoc of his country.

What a pity that Ariosto's charm loses so much in translation! Of all the utopias that sprouted during the Renaissance, *Orlando Furioso* seems to me at once the least pretentious and the wisest. It is harmony itself, a poem that paints and sings while it narrates. It is sheer fantasy, yet everything is as precise and brightly colored as a summer day. "Le donne, i cavalier, l'armi, gli amori" (women, knights, combats, and loves), forever moving in a breathless counterpoint, continually shifting from one enchanting landscape to another, keep us in perpetual suspense. No space ship can be more exciting than the winged horse that leads us to the moon, in search of the lost wits of poets and heroes. As Ariosto himself puts it, in Sir John Harington's classic translation:

> The precious time that fools mis-spend in play,
> the vain attempts that never take effect,
> the vows that sinners make, and never pay,
> the counsels wise that careless men neglect,
> the fond desires that lead us oft astray,
> the praises that with pride the heart infect,
> and all we lose with folly and mis-spending,
> may there be found unto this place ascending.

It is exhilarating to be mad when the whole world has lost its balance. It is comforting, too, to evoke with an admixture of nostalgia and amusement the "gran bontà dei cavalieri antiqui," the unbelievable loyalty of such knights of yore as Rinaldo and Ferraù, who were rivals in love, war, and religion, yet trusted one another enough to ride the same horse in the thick of a forest. Happily, every forest is alive with hermits, giants, magicians, and beautiful girls. Angelica is the fairest of them all, whether she runs away from her glamorous suitors, or awaits, naked and in chains, the monster who would devour her, or yields at last passionately to the humblest and youngest of her admirers. No doubt Ariosto is too urbane, too breezy, to burden Angelica's story with an obvious moral lesson: what rules her adventures is not a Christian love for the deserving poor but a whimsical, pagan Cupid.

Yet the contrast between Angelica's genuine idyl in the natural vegetation of the forest and Armida's bewitched passion in the false background of her magic garden reminds one of the clash between paradise and hell.[14]

Leonardo da Vinci is less humane than Ariosto, no doubt because he is more divine. You cannot describe a god in a few sentences, much less criticize him. Think of the anecdote, reported by Vasari, about the prior of Santa Maria delle Grazie who complained to the duke of Milan because Leonardo took too long completing his painting of the Last Supper. Men of genius, Leonardo replied, "really are doing most when they work least, as they are thinking out ideas"; moreover, it was almost impossible to imagine the features of a man like Judas, "who could resolve to betray his Master, the Creator of the world. . . . But he was willing . . . to search no farther, and for lack of a better model he would use the head of the prior." Let us not behave like the prior. The incomparable artist, the stunning writer, the all-embracing scientist, could not be held to lower his focus from eternity to the burning problems of his time, or to share with his contemporaries the inventions he jotted down in notebooks not meant for publication. Yet when we think of Leonardo's fellow citizen and younger competitor, Michelangelo, who was so deeply involved in the passions of his mortal environment, we can hardly refrain from wondering whether Leonardo, the universal man, did not miss the very things that could have been closest to his heart.

Nevertheless, as a painter, Leonardo brings out certain basic aspects of the transition from the young to the mature Renaissance, coinciding with his own progress from youth to maturity. The frail, pure, unperturbed adolescent girl is gradually displaced as the ideal type of beauty by a more carnal, voluptuous, pensive woman. Just as the linear simplicity of the early profile is now cushioned in shades, so the landscape becomes at once more realistic and complex, and the clear sky is enriched with hazy variations of color and clouds. Let us look first at the earliest painting that has now been definitely ascribed to Leonardo, the *Annunciation* of about 1474. The close observation of nature in the flowers and the angel's birdlike wings already bear witness to Leonardo's scientific realism; but the fine, youthful human figures, the cloudless sky, the artfully arranged trees still belong to the main Quattrocento stream. Slightly later, his *Madonna Benois* has the same smile as Desiderio da Settignano's *Laughing Child;* she might

well seem the mother of that child.[15] But let us move to the famous
Monna Lisa, probably of 1503: all the traits of the mature Renaissance
are there, stressed in artistic perfection.[16] The play of shades character-
izes the full-grown, experienced beauty. The mysterious look and
half-smile hint at a slightly disenchanted self-assurance, and, at the
same time, follow the dictates of fashion, which recommends, in the
words of Angelo Firenzuola, dark brown eyes, a secretive smile, and a
well-rounded hand. The harmonious, yet irregular landscape offers a
gradation of colors, which become hazier with the distance. There is no
room for flowers, but we can find them in artful disorder in the
Madonna of the Rocks at the Louvre, where haze tends to be con-
densed in clouds.

The early Cinquecento presents us with such an exuberance of great
painting that any short account of changing trends and their impact on
the towering personality of the major artists must be inadequate. Still,
a comparison of Raphael's early *Marriage of the Virgin* (1504) with his
Veiled Woman (1516) readily illustrates his evolution from the slim,
youthful grace we have noticed in Leonardo's early paintings to mellow shades and a restrained smile not too unlike *Monna Lisa's.* Again,
the pastoral atmosphere of Correggio's early *Chamber of St. Paul*
becomes frank sensuousness in the so-called *Antiope,* which is more
probably a Venus. What we see is a sultry beauty, who even in her
unsuspecting sleep bears no trace of the frail purity of Botticelli's
Venus; Cupid himself, at her feet, is all flesh. The realistic, luxuriant
foliage and the lurking satyr sharply contrast with Botticelli's stylized
trees and airy wind-god. Correggio moves still closer to uncensored sex
in his *Leda with the Swan.* Whatever doubts Leonardo might have left
on the meaning of the allegory in his earlier painting on the same
subject (of which, unfortunately, only copies have survived) are now
removed.[17]

Let us not say, however, that painters have lost their innocence:
seldom have painters been innocent, and this is probably for the better.
What has changed is not human nature, but the artistic and historical
season: the spring of the Italian Renaissance has gone, and the fruit of
summer is ripe. Adolescent beauty is *passée;* no longer can a girl like
Simonetta enchant a whole city with her silent charm. Though some
historians are still engaged in the improbable defense of the private life
of Lucrezia Borgia, whose experienced beauty attracted so many
princes and poets, no one can deny the profession of Imperia

de'Cugnatis, a young "cortigiana onesta" (should we translate "honorable prostitute?"), who was loved by Raphael and praised by the irreproachable Sadoleto. Still, the only woman whose spell on her contemporaries may perhaps be compared to that of the late Simonetta was mature Vittoria Colonna, first the faithful wife of an unfaithful husband, then the incorruptible guest of a corrupt nunnery. Truly a grand lady, she wrote coldly elegant poems, which give almost no inkling of her quiet despair, and some of the greatest sinners fell platonically in love with her soul.[18]

If spring was not unaware that happiness is fleeting, summer felt more threatened. Some of the young men portrayed by Titian, Giorgione, and Franciabigio look as absorbed in their melancholy as the heroes of Byron. The darkest clouds overshadow the seemingly quiet landscape of Giorgione's *Tempest*. The painting is not dated, and its interpretation is one of the many riddles that make up Giorgione's mystery. But if I may be allowed to intrude the wild speculation of a plain historian where the wise debates of art historians have so far produced no agreement, I would note that Giorgione died in his early thirties, while the Venetian republic of which he was a citizen was fighting for her life against the invading armies of a great coalition. Whatever the artist may have intended to express by inserting in his dramatic landscape a soldier and a nursing, almost disheveled woman, ever so different from the usually placid Virgin-and-Child groups, the images they evoke to my mind, and possibly Giorgione's material models, are a poor peasant woman who has fled from her village and her man standing guard.[19]

It certainly would be imprudent to see in every work of art a direct reference to a precise historical event; but it seems undeniable that, as the political and economic picture became heavier, more tangled and somber, so did the manner of most artists. This holds even for painters like Dosso Dossi or Gerolamo da Carpi, who dodged serious problems for plainly mythological topics or fantasies borrowed from Ariosto. It affects decorative frescoes like those of Moretto in a private mansion of Brescia: here the landscape carries no symbol and the ladies display no thought, but everything is plumper and darker and more intricate than in earlier works of the same kind. As for the three masters we have considered before—Giorgione, Correggio, and Raphael—they all died young, before completing their artistic journey, but there is no doubt about their direction: they were not going to remain forever on the summit of classical balance and harmony they had attained, but they would carry much further their bold experiments in lighting, color, perspective, and motion.

Only two of the giants of the mature Renaissance—Michelangelo and Titian—lived long enough to take part in the third and last Renaissance age and will be with us to the end of our cavalcade. We may temporarily bypass Titian, since his early mood is still close to that of Giorgione, but Michelangelo will not wait. No one else can tell us so much about the spread of the new tendencies from painting to sculpture. For Michelangelo vigorously takes issue with Leonardo, who had gone so far in his praise of painting that he had called it the highest form of science, nobler than poetry, more expressive than music, and more powerful than sculpture. Against this, Michelangelo states that "painting seems to improve in proportion to its leaning towards relief . . . and hence sculpture is its lantern . . . like the sun to the moon." Look at his earliest painting, the *Holy Family,* and you will at once see what he means.[20]

Like Leonardo, Michelangelo defies short description and critical judgment; unlike Leonardo, he soars above his age not by a higher and deeper understanding of Nature, but by a superhuman effort to bend Nature to his will. His pleasures and sorrows, depressions and tensions, are oversize. So are his statues, which tell with terrible intensity what other sculptors feel less strongly or are less capable of conveying. No doubt Michelangelo forced the rebel stone to express many thoughts and symbols that were exclusively his own; but he was neither too aloof nor too eccentric to respond to the general drive of his generation. He too, like the painters we have just observed, departs from the delicate frailty that characterized the art of the late Quattrocento, and matures as he goes. Between his *David,* completed by 1504, and his *Julian,* placed in the Medici chapel some twenty-five years later, there is much the same evolution as between Leonardo's early Madonnas and *Monna Lisa.* The profiles resemble one another, but David is a relatively serene youth, whereas Julian is etched by worries, altogether a tense, mysterious admixture of disenchantment and self-assurance.

Michelangelo's architectural work cannot in its abstraction reflect psychological development so directly, and it seems better to postpone consideration of works which were completed after the mature age of the Renaissance was over. In general, the architects of the early Cinquecento tended to move away from the slender simplicity of the late

Quattrocento. They still strove for harmonious perspective and balance but played more heavily on the alternation of projecting and receding surfaces, which stresses the mass and creates mysterious shades. All this seems in keeping with trends in the figurative arts; it is already evident in San Pietro in Montorio, Bramante's little jewel of 1502, whose shape in blown-up size was to be the heart of St. Peter's original plan. Bramante did not sacrifice grace to power; and even Michelangelo's Sacristia Nuova and Laurentian Library, lightened internally by the traditional color lining of Florentine architecture, still had something in common with the fresher, youthful elegance of Alberti and Laurana. Nothing of that will be left in Michelangelo's St. Peter's, begun in 1547. The plan stems from Bramante, but its realization is a mountain of stone, whose gigantic play of masses needs all the titanic force of Michelangelo not to look inert. Brunelleschi's early Renaissance dome of Santa Maria del Fiore in Florence, with which one cannot help comparing Michelangelo's, was all wings; Michelangelo's is all muscle.

Gigantism has an economic as well as an aesthetic price. Throughout his life Michelangelo was plagued by financial difficulties that hindered his projects; it is true that he did not yield on the amount of his personal reward, which was unusually high for the time. His story, and a few other examples of exceptionally high pay, may have helped entrench among art historians the conviction that the patrons of the Italian Renaissance were lavish, and that they could be lavish because their country was enormously rich. But this is a double fallacy, a confusion between artistic value and economic cost that no economic historian ought to allow. Even Quattrocento Italy, though probably better off than most other countries, was not as affluent as she had been in the time of Giotto and Dante. The end of the fifteenth century witnessed a chain of bank failures in the major financial centers of Venice and Florence. The wars of the early Cinquecento drained her resources at a frightful rate: cities were burned and plundered, the best land was "stripped bare, torn, and overrun," commerce was hampered, artisans were thrown out of work and often forced to run away, and the propertied classes were oppressed by heavy taxation and ransoms of every kind.

Even today, and without a major declared war, our expenditure for art is a tiny fraction of our military expenses; the cost of government also is very high. Likewise, the wars and the amusements of Renaissance princes absorbed an incomparably larger proportion of their budget than did their patronage of the arts. The size of Michelangelo's earnings was as abnormal as that of his works. Philip II delayed payment on so many of Titian's paintings that the unfortunate artist lost count of them. Isabella d'Este, the most prominent patroness and art collector in the mature Renaissance, haggled like a rug merchant over each piece she committed to hard-pressed artists; her brothers made Ariosto earn his keep by hard administrative work. Actually, before the Council of Trent it was often possible to hire a writer with no outlay of cash by giving him an ecclesiastic benefice without ecclesiastic duties. Above all, the salary of the poet and the painter is virtually the only outlay required for a poem or painting; not much marble is necessary for a sculpture; and though the Renaissance erected a good number of churches and palaces, they usually were much smaller than the cathedrals and castles of the Middle Ages, and the investment of material and manpower was proportionately smaller. Michelangelo's colossal St. Peter's is practically the only exception.[21]

The exception, however, proved too expensive for the ordinary resources of Pope Leo X, who resorted to the usual source the Holy See tapped to raise money in a hurry—granting a special indulgence to all those who would pay for the good work of building to God the largest shrine in history. He did not foresee that a German monk, who doubted that good works could supplement faith as a means of salvation, would be provoked to raise the standard of rebellion; nor did he realize, even later, that Luther's revolt would tear apart the Catholic community. Thus the cost of the only Renaissance church that was bigger than any medieval cathedral turned out to be staggering; Rome is still paying for it. No doubt indulgences were not the whole issue: there were theological differences, hostility to papal absolutism, resentment against a corrupt establishment. These problems, however, were not new, and Catholic unity had long survived them. What precipitated the split and prevented a prompt mending was chiefly the growing cultural distance between Italian elite and German mass. Few were the men who, like Sadoleto and Erasmus, Melanchthon and Contarini, could bridge the gap. Their renown was great but their views did not prevail.[22]

In the crucial years of the mature Renaissance, Rome was too engrossed in her own artistic and literary achievements to pay adequate attention to Luther's anguish. In 1516, one year before Luther nailed his theses on the church door at Wittenberg, Pietro Pomponazzi, the highest paid professor of philosophy in Italy, published an essay which maintained that the immortality of the soul could neither be proved nor disproved, but that man should avoid sin not for the hope of salvation but in order to make himself a god rather than a beast. The Patriarch of Venice burned the book, but the University of Bologna gave Pomponazzi a raise, and Leo X thoroughly enjoyed the ensuing scholarly discussion.[23] Luther's diatribes did not interest the pope enough to make him set aside his intellectual and political pursuits; when he finally reacted, he entrusted the rebuttal not to the subtlest theologians but to the most elegant humanists, Cajetan and Aleandro. Note that Cajetan had preceded Pomponazzi in asserting that Aristotle taught that the soul is mortal. The misunderstanding was not entirely new. Had the great Roman emperors, Trajan and Marcus Aurelius, not dismissed Christianity as a vulgar superstition? Was it really necessary for a glorious culture to worry about the emotions of lower people? Renaissance Rome woke up to the danger sooner than had ancient Rome; but the delay was sufficient to transform what art historians still call "the age of Leo X" into the age of Luther. Thus, paradoxically, the greatest period of Italian art not only coincided with political bankruptcy but was encompassed between two missed opportunities: at the beginning, America became Spanish, and at the end, Germany became Protestant.

Perhaps the best conclusion of our breathless survey of artistic and literary maturity is Machiavelli's poetical dialogue with the capricious goddess who escaped his grasp, "Occasion" (that is, Fortune):[24]

> — O tell me who you are! such graceful springs
> no mortal woman, I believe, can match.
> Why don't you stop? why do your feet have wings?

> — I am Occasion, whom few people meet;
> it is my fate always to shift, because
> over a wheel I hold one of my feet.

> Nobody flies as fast as I can run,
> but I have wings to hide from everyone
> the secret of my speed till I have gone.

> My breast, my face I cover with my hair,
> whose scanty yarn is gathered on my front,
> to keep me from detection when I am there.

Behind my front there is no hair at all:
no man whom I have passed can grab me again,
none overtake me, should I turn and call.

— But after you, who is coming at slow pace?
— She is Regret; therefore do mark my words:
whoever misses me, must her embrace.

You too, who talking precious time so spend
in your pursuit of thoughts distant and vain,
you do not see, alas, nor understand

that I have gone from you beyond recall!

IV Decline   1527–1559

HE WORDS of Leonardo, "While I thought that I was learning how to live, I have been learning how to die" could apply to any age, for every age carries the germs of its own destruction; but they fit most particularly the third age of the Italian Renaissance, which was so full of artistic vitality, yet so inexorably slipping toward its own demise. When did it become clear that the better days were over?

Political history offers more than one date. Every turn of the screw was followed by fits of resistance. The crushing defeat of Francis I at Pavia (1525) ought to have persuaded the Italians that France was a broken reed, and that there was no escape from the overwhelming power of Charles V, emperor, king of Spain, lord of the Low Countries, sovereign of southern Italy, and suzerain of the northern duchy of Milan. Yet the Venetians made a belated try at breaking the encirclement, with the solid asset of their undefeated fleet, the dubious assistance of the pope, and the vain hope of French help. More ominously, in 1527 the sack of Rome by unpaid Spanish soldiers and German mercenaries (the latter, mostly Lutheran) dispelled the aura of inviolability surrounding the Holy See, and seemed to renew the atrocities which had delivered ancient Rome to the barbarians. Still, the French kept challenging the Spaniards, Venice fought on, Genoa recovered her long-lost independence through a political turnabout of the Genoese mercenary admiral, Andrea Doria. Florence, too, rid herself once more of the Medici, who had been recalled fifteen years earlier, and restored her traditional republic. Not for long: by 1530 the Medici pope,

Clement VII, forced by Charles V to play down the recent disaster in
Rome, to crown him emperor, and to forbid Henry VIII to annul
his marriage with the emperor's aunt (thus forfeiting the allegiance of
England) had obtained as a sop the help of the imperial troops to
enthrone the Medici as dukes of Florence. This was almost the end of
Italian hopes, but not of calamities. In 1538 a Venetian fleet, abandoned
by its imperial allies in the midst of a battle, was crushed by the Turks;
Venice lost her tranquillity at sea, though not her courage. As late as
1554–55 republican Siena defended her liberty heroically against an
imperial besieging army; when she fell, a handful of Sienese and
Florentine exiles held out for another four years in the castle of
Montalcino. Finally, in 1559, the peace of Cateau-Cambrésis sealed the
fate of Italy: the Spaniards were entrenched as masters throughout the
south and in the heart of the northern plain; all the surviving Italian
states, except Venice and rugged Piedmont, bent more or less deeply
under the supremacy of Spain.[1]

Ironically, economic conditions tended to improve as resistance fal-
tered and fighting abated; but it is hard to assess the size of a recovery
which was unevenly distributed and, even at its peak, nowhere complete. Perhaps the only generalized indication of resiliency lies in the
population figures: the majority of available urban statistics show a
sharp upward turn after 1527. Florence remains almost stationary, but
Venice increases by more than 50 per cent in fifty years, and Pavia,
once the siege and battle of 1524–25, the seven-day French sack of 1527,
and the plague of the same year have passed, more than doubles her
population in fifteen years. Sparse figures for the open country suggest
similar trends, notably in Sicily, which has been relatively spared by
war throughout the Cinquecento.[2] Demographic survival and growth,
however, may engender overpopulation and depression as easily as they
can stimulate economic development.

Development had occurred during the commercial revolution of
the Middle Ages, when a combination of correlated drives had caused
the population and the standard of living to climb simultaneously, on
parallel tracks. A large amount of uncultivated or inadequately ex-
ploited land had been brought under culture; new markets had been
opened to Italian trade; better tools and business techniques had been
introduced; credit had swollen the resources of the money economy; a
freer society had favored initiative, increased the number and appetites
of the consumers, and quickened the transmission of new methods and

ideas. All these drives had lost impetus by the mid-fourteenth century, when the initial fuel, population growth, dried up. They had dwindled further during the demographic decline and economic crises of the next hundred years. Yet some of them were still at work in the youthful age of the Renaissance, when demographic and economic stabilization made a moderate recovery possible. Had there been no invasions, the mature Renaissance might have seen the resumption of demographic growth and started a new chain reaction. Unfortunately, the trend was reversed thirty or forty years too late, when the battered society of the declining Renaissance wanted rest more than expansion and found the surplus of people a burden rather than a challenge.[3]

To a much greater degree than the opening years of the Renaissance, the closing years offered opportunities to a well-entrenched elite but not to the mass. Still, Italy in the Cinquecento was not yet too weary to respond to a favorable conjuncture; indeed, after the peace of 1559 was consolidated, her economy would head for a second spell of Indian summer, a pale repetition of the Indian summer of the early Renaissance. Before and after 1559, the basic assets and liabilities remained the same: on the positive side, a higher degree of urbanization, mechanization, financial liquidity, and social mobility than in the rest of Europe; on the negative side, soil exhaustion, industrial conservatism, commercial timidity, and other tokens of a mature economy that has passed its prime. All liabilities were more conspicuous in the normally poorer south: by 1532, when Pedro de Toledo was appointed viceroy of Naples, the trade of the kingdom was virtually monopolized by northern Italians, barons and brigands vied in oppressing the peasants, and large stretches of overcropped land had been abandoned to sheep. The enlightened energy of the Spanish viceroy gave some relief to the capital, which began its somewhat pathological growth as an urban metropolis without industries or trades. The rest of the kingdom, fleeced by excessive taxation, continued to decline, still exporting foodstuffs because the peasants did not eat enough. Rome also grew, the pope being her principal industry, but most of the papal states were not much better off than the southern kingdom. Without taking such a deep plunge, the formerly wealthy cities of Tuscany failed to pick up. Pisa and Siena were ruined beyond repair, Lucca was hit by the bankruptcy of seven among her major merchant companies between 1520 and 1552, Florence held on to the remainder of her financial power but was almost wiped out as the main center of the woolen industry.⁴

Northern Italy, however, managed much better. The fertile Po valley and its sizable urban centers made a remarkable comeback from the disasters caused by nearly three decades of fighting on her soil. Here agricultural techniques were more progressive and industries more diversified than in any other part of Europe. Still more stunning was the surge of Genoa after Andrea Doria cut her ties with France, in 1528, and made her the chief provider of ships and loans for Charles V and Philip II. Long before 1528, a number of Genoese entrepreneurs had infiltrated the key business centers of the Iberian peninsula and its oversea dependencies; in the fifty years that followed, they concentrated in their hands the most profitable branches of trade in the Spanish empire, took a lion's share of the imports of American gold and silver, and became the strongest financiers in the entire Catholic world. No less astonishing was the continuing prosperity of Venice, in spite of Portuguese competition in the Asian and African trade, of Turkish encroachments on her colonial possessions, and of her own heightened military expenses. While defending with a good measure of success their traditional strong points—the Mediterranean sea trade, trade with the German hinterland, the industrial arts of glass and silk —the Venetians also expanded their investments in other directions. They trebled in thirty years the output of their fledgling woolen industry and stepped up their agricultural production through better techniques and the reclamation of marshy land. Northern Italy, however, shared with the south certain handicaps: luxury industry and trade outweighed the production of, and trade in, cheaper goods for mass consumption; the emigration of craftsmen and merchants, driven out by political and religious strife or attracted by the hope of greater gains, deprived the country of skills and capital and this made the competition of foreign countries more damaging.⁵

Even as the economic center of gravity was shifting from the peninsula proper to northern Italy, where it still lies today, the focus of intellectual and artistic activity also drifted northward. In the youthful age of the Renaissance, Florence had easily maintained the leadership she had held ever since the time of Dante and Giotto; but in the mature age, only the overwhelming stature of Leonardo, Michelangelo, and Machiavelli could offset the fact that the greatest poet, Ariosto, and three of the greatest painters, Giorgione, Titian, and Correggio, were northern Italians. In the second quarter of the Cinquecento, Venice and her domains were definitely more creative than Florence and Tuscany in architecture, painting, and literature. Nevertheless, it was at this time that the Florentine vernacular finally won its long battle for recognition as the newest classic language, on a par with classic Latin and classic Greek. The decisive push in its favor, however, came from Venetian Pietro Bembo, not a great writer but an elegant imitator of the classics, a highly respected critic and grammarian, and a member of the social elite. His friendship with Aldo Manuzio and other printers who made Venice Europe's greatest publishing center helped him propagate uniform spelling rules. Bembo insisted that the standard language should be neither the living Florentine speech of a Machiavelli, nor the basically Tuscan speech which northerners like Ariosto and Castiglione had enriched with expressions from other regions, but the model set by Petrarch and Boccaccio two hundred years earlier. Such a prescription was bound to meet with considerable and spirited opposition: it satisfied nobody's municipal pride, and it bolstered the tendency of Italian intellectuals to talk above the head of their readers, a tendency that is still visible today. But this is precisely why Bembo's formula triumphed after a long struggle. The Italians would not take dictation from the living language of any town or literary circle; a standard safely enshrined in the past fitted the aristocratic aloofness of the elite.[6]

Nevertheless, the aging Renaissance did not have the unanimous, naïve reverence for classic models that prevailed in the Quattrocento. The pompousness of formal writers, their single-minded worship of Petrarch, and their pedantry in rejecting whatever might disagree with ancient canons of style provoked an increased production of parody and roguery. The language ranges from the so-called macaroni Latin to colloquial Florentine and the funniest combinations of coarse northern dialects. There are a few gems scattered amid much rubbish: for instance, a few pages of the overpraised autobiography of Benvenuto Cellini; some lively, multidialectal scenes of popular life in the plays of Padua-born Ruzzante, a professional actor and forerunner of the *commedia dell'arte;* some realistic vignettes of peasants and rural landscapes in the pig-Latin poems of Teofilo Folengo, a lazy monk from Mantua; and the witty parodies of Petrarchist lyrics by Florentine

Francesco Berni, such as the following catalogue of the beautiful features of his beloved:

> Silvery hair, unbending as it twists
> in artless shape around a golden face;
> fair, wavy brow, where Love and Death in vain
> seek for their shots a proper landing place;
> white, pearly eyes, cross-fire that will not meet
> the look of anyone but their own kind;
> milk-colored lips, and you, gripping my mind,
> fingers and hands so sweetly fat and short . . .

Still, roguery is not social protest, parody is not political satire. Once again we may be surprised at the amount of ink that was spilled on literary problems while Italy was burning. Once again, too, we have to remind ourselves that the priorities of the Renaissance were those of an elite which regarded artistic and literary glory as the supreme earthly achievement. Even as Matteo Palmieri had announced in the Quattrocento "a new age, full of hope and promise" because Latin had recovered its purity, so the Cinquecento writers who hammered down the rules of Italian grammar and style felt that they were preparing for their country a better future. They were not as visionary as one might think at first. Italy as a nation, it is still often claimed, was not the product of geography or history but rather of literature: her image was created by the Latin poets of the golden age, then refurbished by the Tuscan poets of the Middle Ages. If this is essentially true, as I believe it is, the final attainment of literary unity under the flag of classic Tuscan was the most significant step toward nationhood that Renaissance Italy was able to take, even if it widened the split between written and spoken language.

No other Italian dialect could have offered an alternative to Tuscan. Rome never was the birthplace of much literature, whether in antiquity or in the Renaissance: Virgil was Mantuan like Folengo, Livy was Paduan like Ruzzante, and almost none of the literary celebrities who surrounded the popes were Roman natives. Moreover, the moral and material credit of the popes hit a low point between the sack of Rome and the take-off of the Counter-Reformation. Venice enjoyed a greater prestige, but she was as peripheral to Italy as England, at a later period, to Europe: she was half-tied to her oversea dominions, and her institutions were too peculiar to bear transplantation. They were imitated to some extent in Genoa and Lucca, the two other republics that survived beyond 1559, and they were highly praised by political writers both from Venice and other Italian states: Giannotti, Contarini, Garimberti, and others. But neither Venice nor Rome looked like usable models to the greatest political thinker of the time, Francesco Guicciardini.[7]

Guicciardini, a Florentine like his elder contemporary and correspondent, Machiavelli, has often been compared with him, usually unfavorably.[8] The debate cannot be settled, for it is swayed by largely irrelevant judgments of value. Curiously, those who praise Machiavelli most highly for having divorced politics from morality cannot forgive Guicciardini for taking the next logical step and forbidding the emotions of his heart to interfere with the intuition of his mind. Yet Machiavelli's warning to princes, that if they have to choose between being loved or feared they should prefer to be feared, is hardly less cynical and altogether crueler than Guicciardini's admonition: "Do all you can to seem good, for this will help you in numberless ways; but since false reputations do not last, you will find it hard to seem good for long unless you are really good." The difference between Machiavelli's mingling of idealism with realism and Guicciardini's bitter pragmatism reflects less a discrepancy in temperament than a change of circumstances. Machiavelli wrote when the political fate of Italy was not finally decided and hence could indulge in generous illusions; Guicciardini, when all hopes for liberation from foreign and domestic tyranny were shattered. At that late moment the best one could do was to protect the private interest of individual citizens, and Guicciardini justified any means that would further that aim. As if to compensate for the pettiness of this assumption, he displayed an unusually broad conception of Italy as a potential nation. While Machiavelli in his *Florentine History* saw the whole country as an extension of his native city, Guicciardini in his *History of Italy*—note the difference in the title—strove for impartiality. He did not expect, like Machiavelli, that the puny Italian states could profit from the example of ancient Rome: donkeys cannot gallop like horses, he said. But he did depict the balance of Italian powers prevailing in the late Quattrocento as a lost paradise of prosperity and peace; this, too, was an unrealistic, idealized vision of the past.[9]

On a lower level, Monsignor Della Casa's little book of good manners, *Galateo,* is often compared with Castiglione's *Courtier,* also usually unfavorably, and for the same irrelevant considerations that work against Guicciardini. Della Casa's unpretentious treatise was published only a few months before the peace of Cateau-Cambrésis, which buried all chances for civic activity and heroic posture. Although people still liked to read about virtuous courtiers and brave knights-errant, in real life the former would have been misfits and the latter plainly ridiculous. By striving to guard private individuals against commonplace vulgarity, arrogance, or tactlessness, Monsignor Della Casa rendered to society a modest, but genuine service. "People," he said, "fear wild beasts and are unafraid of mosquitoes and flies; yet they complain mostly of the latter, because they are continuously molested by them. . . . Hence, whoever plans to live not in deserts or hermitages, but in towns and among fellow-men, ought to learn how to be graceful and agreeable in behavior and manners." It would be bad manners for us to chide him for providing no ammunition against wild beasts, but merely a witty insecticide. Nevertheless, we are taken aback when, in a supplementary treatise on the best behavior of inferiors toward their superiors, Monsignor Della Casa recommends total obsequiousness, unencumbered by shame, and backs his advice with the following example: "The more ashamed a prostitute feels, the less she is worth; for it is her profession in return for money to satisfy whoever asks her. Hence, if she is ashamed, though this is in itself a commendable feeling, she becomes less proficient in her profession." [10]

Actually, the mid-sixteenth century was about as permissive toward professional sex as the mid-twentieth toward unprofessional premarital experience. A Milanese lawyer, who evidently was conversant with the Reformation, argued that a prostitute should not be harassed, because "you cannot avoid sin by your works but only by the grace of God." Although in Florence even a "cortigiana onesta" was required to wear a yellow veil, much as the Jews had to wear a yellow badge, when beautiful Tullia d'Aragona was caught without the veil, Duke Cosimo de'Medici pardoned her "because she is a poet." Her poems, oozing Platonic and Petrarchist love, are neither better nor worse than those of her poet friends, among whom we find some of the best people: Molza, Varchi, Pietro Bembo. We do not have to pick up the invidious rumor that her lovers paid her in ghost writing: she had some learning and distinction, and if she repeated conventional themes in elegant wrapping, this was a common characteristic of nearly all the overflowing poetical production of the declining Renaissance, whether lyrical, epic, or tragic. If we look for deeper emotion, we must turn to the sloppy, but musical poems of another woman, probably not a courtesan but an unwise lover—Gaspara Stampa. Her inspiration was as fickle as her heart, but it dictated a few touching expressions of bliss and despair:

> Let us together live a joyful life
> until the sun of our eyes goes out. . . .
> We shall sing with the birds all our love!

or, in a spell of repentance:

> Lord, who redeemed the seed of all mankind,
> o my sweet Lord, don't suffer that I die!

or, in love again:

> All my delights and all my sports are these:
> to live in flame, and yet to feel no pain.[11]

Higher and more complex emotions underlie the harsh, often obscure poems of Michelangelo. Here we shall cite only the brief reply he sent to a flatterer who had ascribed to his statue, *Night,* the desire of being awakened in order to prove that she was really alive:

> 'Tis good to sleep and more to be of stone
> while all is ruin, all is burning shame.
> Not to see, not to hear fortune I name;
> therefore don't wake me up, do leave me alone.

One cannot forever wear mourning for the lost freedom of one's fatherland. Some ten years later, Michelangelo was to write the king of France, one of the invaders of Italy, who had requested his services, a letter humble enough to please Monsignor Della Casa. No matter: his sculpture does tell a story of artistic, religious, and political torment. It is enough to compare the contained, harmonious *Pietà* of St. Peter's in Rome with the desolate, twisted *Pietà* of Santa Maria del Fiore in Florence to realize the change in his personality from the beginning of the Cinquecento to the final demise of the Renaissance fifty years later. This tension and distortion, and similar tendencies of other artists who died during the Renaissance age of maturity or survived into the age of decline, have recently been classified by many historians of art under the heading of "mannerism." So be it, if the term mannerism is used as an arbitrary label for any kind of deviation from the heroic, classic, or realistic poise of the early and high Renaissance. But if mannerism is taken in its original meaning of art "after the manner" of somebody else, stating that Raphael, Correggio, Michelangelo, or Titian gradually inclined toward mannerism makes no more sense than saying that the models gradually came to resemble their imitators.[12]

Undoubtedly, some of the veritable mannerists had original talent: Parmigianino, to mention only one instance, is not merely an imitator of Correggio but has his own personality and charm, no matter whether or not his long-necked Madonna should be regarded as a bridge toward the elongated figures of El Greco, and whether or not the dramatic change of his personality was triggered by his harrowing experience in the sack of Rome. In our context, however, we are more interested in the long-run evolution of the great master whose tireless activity spanned the second and third ages of the Renaissance and went even beyond it—Titian. By the mid-sixteenth century, the Venetian school of painting, of which he was the central figure, had taken the lead; it was to retain its creativity long after the other Italian schools. No doubt Titian was not as involved as Michelangelo in the political and moral problems of his time. At most, one might suggest that his patriotism unconsciously manifested itself in the contrast between the idealized features of his Venetian doges, Antonio Grimani and Andrea Gritti, and the unflattering portraits of foreign rulers such as Charles V, Philip II, and Francis I, to say nothing of his scathing pictorial denunciation of Pope Paul III and his family. The contrast, however, was not invented by Titian; nor did his merciless realism stop the emperor or the pope from commissioning his paintings and being grateful for them. There is, moreover, no such sharp difference between early and late works as we observed in Michelangelo. Old age made the master's stroke less firm and blurred the details of his outlines, but it did not tarnish the splendor of his color or render his late paintings consistently gloomier than the early, Giorgionesque ones. Like Venice herself, Titian never gave in.

Still, the historian, ever on the lookout for his game, cannot help seeking through Titian's works a trace of the changing trends and moods of his epoch. The portraits will not do for this purpose. We may learn something more from three successive allegories, whose subjects and meaning have not been conclusively identified and need not be discussed here. The first of them, of about 1515, represents a woman in her prime, who looks at herself in a mirror held before her by a beguiled gentleman, while another mirror shines at her back. Her full, carnal beauty agrees with the ideal of the mature Renaissance as expressed by the almost contemporary *Monna Lisa* of Leonardo and *Veiled Woman* of Raphael; the fact that she looks more voluptuous than the latter and less enigmatic than the former depends on the extrovert sensuality of Titian. The second allegory, probably of 1532, is more complex and brooding. Both the gentleman and the lovely woman are absorbed in tender melancholy; the glowing mirror has been replaced by a transparent sphere, probably a symbol of fortune's fragility, and the solid wall in the background now opens onto a stormy landscape; a compassionate lady offers her sympathy, and a sweet Cupid presents his arrows. The third allegory, of about 1560, converts the sad composure of the second allegory into a busy and almost coarse scheme. The delicate woman in love has become an impudent, somewhat flabby Venus; the caressing gentleman, a lurking winged boy; Cupid is blindfolded and writhing; the demure, charitable lady has turned to a half-naked procuress; the stormy landscape has almost crowded out the wall. From self-satisfied balance to deep dejection and from dejection to disenchanted unbalance: do not the three paintings fit three successive stages of the mature and declining Renaissance? [13]

The mood of decline, however, is variable and hard to define. Youth and maturity knew what they wanted, or, at least, what they hoped; old age wavers among conflicting goals. The political and religious outlook is almost unrelieved distress, but the economy is beginning to pick up again; arts and letters, after climbing to what seemed the highest standard of perfection, are exploring formulas that might avoid repetitiousness without leaving the heights. The narcissism of the late Quattrocento is definitely gone, but the very admiration shown by the invaders for the superior culture of Italy encourages complacency, and where hope seems to be unrealistic, one can still try escape. Nowhere is the presence of contradictory drives more evident than in architecture, although its abstract values, as usual, cannot be translated directly into the language of history. Here the clash between a still vigorous longing for classic balance and an irresistible craving for new emotional, intellectual, or merely whimsical expressions was especially sharp and productive. This was partly the consequence of a lag in the development of the art during the years when war and economic distress had restricted the investment of capital and manpower in expensive building. Renaissance architecture reached maturity while the Renaissance as a whole was sailing into old age; hence its most poised forms got enmeshed with restless ones, often conceived by the same man. Michele Sanmicheli, for instance, took picturesque liberties with classic proportions and shapes in the gateways of his native Verona around 1540; then, about 1550, he adopted for the Palazzo Grimani in Venice an impeccable balance of superposed classic orders.

By that time Andrea Palladio had begun the construction of his most famous works, the Basilica of Vicenza and the Rotonda in the rural vicinity. He continued for another thirty years to build stately mansions and villas which combined the most scrupulous observance of the classic rules of balance and style with a Venetian and almost manneristic taste for rhythmic chromaticism. Initially a protégé of Giorgio Trissino, an ultraconservative nobleman who sided with the emperor against Venice in the years of her greatest peril, Palladio had been indoctrinated by him to stick to the classics. But Trissino produced only stilted tragedy and stillborn epics, whereas Palladio created a series of gems—first of all, because he had genius, but also because architecture can be moving without getting as passionate as poetry. Moreover, the atmosphere of the Venetian hinterland, sheltered from war and nursed by the sound economic administration of the Most Serene Republic, was congenial to Palladio's quiet harmony and unruffled movement. In other parts of Italy, where the scars were still open, the shift from Renaissance proper to early mannerism was more of a break. There is a striking difference between the Palazzo della Farnesina (1512) and the Palazzo Massimo (1532), built in Rome by the same architect, Baldassare Peruzzi of Siena: the former still preserves the linear purity of the early Renaissance; the latter displays the irregular shape and chromatic movement that usher in a more tormented age. The Palazzo Marino, built by Galeazzo Alessi in Milan (1557-58), is still more unorthodox. Only the classic columns of the ground floor remind us that chronologically we are still in the Renaissance; the colorful exuberance of the ornamentation belongs to mannerism.

When we speak of "decline of the Renaissance," we do not necessarily imply a judgment of value, but merely an acknowledgment that a certain style and way of life, chiefly among the elite, were disintegrating. We can prove or, at least, contend that the republican government offered more liberty to a larger number of Florentines than the ducal government by Cosimo de'Medici, or that a majority of the Milanese had a higher standard of living under the Sforza dukes than under the Spanish governors; but there are no quantitative or objective tests that will demonstrate the superiority of balance over movement, elegance over grandeur, Renaissance over baroque. We may have our personal preferences, but we no longer recognize absolute canons of classic perfection. And even if we limit ourselves to intellectual and artistic creativity, we must concede that weariness in certain fields was compensated for by a new fertility in others. At most we may distinguish between viable innovation and aimless change. The distinction is never easy to draw, but perhaps we can take as our guide an allegorical dream of Ruzzante, where the genial playwright exalts Joy, "who never stands still because she would like to sing, dance, pick flowers, and pick up a good fight, all at once," but deplores Caprice, "who never has rest, is not where he is and would like to be where he is not, wishes to be someone else and not to be himself." [14]

Even before Ruzzante's death in 1542, professional troupes had been sprouting in the Venetian region and elsewhere, spreading along their trail the jokes, the inventions, and the masks of the *commedia dell'arte,* a very old craft that was to attain its full bloom after the end of the Renaissance. Similarly, music, which ever since the beginning of the Renaissance had been widely appreciated in Italy but depended mostly on the talent of foreign artists, now became a typical Italian forte, with its principal centers in Venice and Rome. Opera came only in the second half of the century, and so did Palestrina's best works. But they were preceded by a sudden output of compositions of all kinds, ranging from homophony to polyphony, from popular *frottole* and literary madrigals to the most solemn liturgical compositions, while Nicola Vicentino's *Ancient Music Converted to Modern Practice* (1555) challenged the old canons of style. The short story, too, got a second wind in the concluding period of the Renaissance. It did not quite recover the sublime heights of Boccaccio, but it supplied an infinite variety of plots to Spanish, French, and English dramatists, including, of course, Shakespeare. With much smaller merit of its own, a book of emblems (symbolic figures with explanatory devices), written by Andrea Alciato, a great jurist who indulged in erudite hobbies, inspired a later generation of English metaphysical poets.

What we have called the old age of the Italian Renaissance displayed a new and almost revolutionary creativity in science. What progress had occurred in the two earlier periods had largely been a by-product of something else: geographical discoveries had served the quest for economic gain; perspective and anatomy had been pursued by painters and sculptors seeking artistic truth. Leonardo himself had cultivated science as a lonesome, self-contained genius. His scientific notes and drawings were not prepared for publication, and it is an open question whether Brussels-born Vesalius saw the drawings before preparing his epoch-making anatomic treatise at the University of Padua (1543). The scholars of the mid-sixteenth century, however, carried their discussions into the open and used the press to gain glory from their findings. Fracastoro's books on syphilis and contagion appeared in 1530 and 1546; Vannuccio Biringuccio's manual, *Pyrotechnic* (that is, explosives, mining, and metallurgy), in 1540; Gabriele Falloppia's *Anatomic Observations* in 1561. Science had come to its own. Without trying to follow it up in all its ramifications, let us linger a moment on the curious contest between two Lombard mathematicians, Fontana of Brescia and Cardano of Pavia.

In 1537 Nicola Fontana, nicknamed Tartaglia ("the stammerer") because a French soldier plundering Brescia had mutilated his tongue, published his *Nova Scientia,* which dealt with gunnery and took an important step toward a correct law of falling bodies. An engraving of the book shows the author proudly surrounded by Plato, Aristotle, Euclid, and the mathematical sciences personified. Later, Tartaglia found the solution of cubic equations but made the mistake of communicating it under the seal of secrecy to an unscrupulous competitor, Gerolamo Cardano. In 1545 the latter published Tartaglia's formula in his *Ars Magna,* and added to it the solution of quartic equations, found by a former servant of his. The dispute between Tartaglia's "new science" and Cardano's "great art" took the theatrical form of scientific challenges, with a flurry of cartels and countercartels—the latest hangover of the nostalgia for knights that had engendered *Orlando Furioso.* For all these chivalresque trappings, both Tartaglia and Cardano were self-made men. Cardano had a faster, if more checkered career, because he seasoned with a dash of quackery his outstanding talents in every scientific and parascientific field: he gained fame as mathematician, physicist, physician, philosopher, astrologer, and magician. He also tried to help his luck by gambling, a fitting industry when other economic activities entailed considerable risks. The by-product was a remarkable little book, which contained the earliest systematic computations of mathematical probabilities. Fortune, however, deserted him in his old age. His two sons were worse rascals than the father; one of them was executed for poisoning his wife, who had well deserved that fate. Then, in 1570, the aged professor was arrested under charges of heresy, forced to recant, forbidden to publish books, and deprived of his chair at the University of Bologna—the very university that fifty years earlier had given a raise to Pomponazzi for doubting philosophically the immortality of the soul.[15]

The end of religious permissiveness was the most telling blow among those which hastened the Italian Renaissance to its grave; but one might also reverse the statement and contend that religious permissiveness ended because the weary Renaissance became more mindful of death. So long as people were convinced of man's ability to lift himself up to the level of angels, the age-old problem of moral corruption did not call for total and immediate reformation. Every individual could work his own salvation, every clergyman could administer grace-giving sacraments, repentance was acceptable even in the last hour, and the day of judgment for the whole ecclesiastic and lay society was known only to God. Still, the first ten years after the papal condemnation of Luther in 1520 brought about increased devotion in Italy, both through personal worship and good works and through the good example of special groups, such as the Capuchins, the Theatines, the Barnabites, and other religious communities, whose goal was not a reexamination of theology but a restoration of morals and discipline. To what extent this movement was a response to German protest rather than an upshot of preexisting Italian anxiety is a debated and probably insoluble question. In the Middle Ages already, moral self-reformation, without dogmatic change, had checked the progress of theological dissent and saved the unity of the Catholic Church. This time, however, house cleaning lacked the support of a pope like Gregory VII or a saint like Francis of Assisi. Only one pope, Hadrian VI—a misunderstood and misunderstanding stranger, the only non-Italian pontiff of the Renaissance—was willing to begin self-reformation from the top: "No wonder," he said, "that the disease has descended from the head to the limbs, from the pope to the prelates . . . and clergymen. . . . Let each of us judge himself, instead of waiting for God's judgment in the day of wrath."[16]

Hadrian died shortly afterward, in 1523. The inaction of other popes moved a lukewarm believer, Guicciardini, to reflect that, had personal interests not obliged him to work for the aggrandizement of the pontiffs, he would have loved Martin Luther more than himself. Not that he wished to be loosed from the traditional laws of Christianity, but only a Luther could either force the priests to behave or throw the rascals out. Indeed, the mounting feeling that few men really could or would lift themselves up to the level of angels, and the clandestine diffusion of Protestant literature—again, we cannot disentangle external influences from internal despondency—led many religious Italians to turn their attention from disciplinary to theological problems. There was no rigid partition as yet between Lutheran tenets and Catholic orthodoxy. As early as 1523 Gaspare Contarini, the future cardinal, wrote a friend: "Nobody can justify himself through his works; we must take shelter in grace, and grace is obtained through faith in Christ." As late as 1546 Gerolamo Seripando, another future cardinal, urged the Council of Trent to endorse the compromise theory of man's double justification, through his own prayer and through faith.

These and other quasi-Protestant statements by prominent Catholics were not merely counsels of expediency; they stemmed from the profound conviction that the "separate brothers" beyond the Alps were not too far from the worried but obedient sons of Rome. Nor was it only to escape punishment that so many Italian dissenters toned down their expressions and played on ambiguity as long as they could. When they could not, they emigrated to Protestant countries; but even there most of them had to dissimulate or to wander farther and farther apart from their native land. For Protestantism in its early days was more intolerant than Catholicism, and few Italians were ready to accept the stern and seemingly irrational discipline of a distant, terrible, transcendent God.

We cannot follow here the vicissitudes of the Italian religious exiles, whose departures were an even greater loss to their country than those of the equally numerous political refugees and economic *émigrés*. Italy was richer in businessmen, artists, and politicians than in committed consciences. People tend to forget, nowadays, that Italian exiles were the founding fathers of Unitarianism, one of the most tolerant and rationalistic branches of the reformed faith. Toleration and reason, however, fare badly in times of violent struggle. The time for peaceful coexistence of elegant corruption with kind love was over, as was the age of blood-sparing mercenaries, snobbish courtiers, and republican humanists. It is no mere accident that Lucca, the last surviving "governo largo" (that is, relatively democratic republic), was now simultaneously driven to let her great citizen, Francesco Burlamacchi, be executed for advocating the restoration of republican government throughout Tuscany, to ease into exile her prominent heretics by tipping them off on impending arrest, and to become gradually a still closer oligarchy than Genoa or Venice. Meanwhile, chances for a reconciliation between moderate Protestants and moderate Catholics dwindled. Pope Paul III, elected in 1534, took the first serious steps to make the Roman church more severe, both toward its own abuses and toward religious dissent. The moderates enthusiastically endorsed the first part of the program, but the second part played into the hands of their adversaries. The most important moves were the recognition of the Society of Jesus, the stiffening of the Inquisition in the new vest of the Roman Holy Office, and, in 1545, the opening of the Council of Trent, which yielded nothing to the demands of the dissenters. The last hopes for moderation were doomed ten years later, when seventy-nine-year-old Cardinal Carafa, the grand inquisitor, became pope under the name of Paul IV.[17]

If a single person were to be charged with dealing the final stroke to the declining Renaissance, Paul IV would be the most likely one. A nearly paranoiac man, who boasted to the Venetian ambassador that if his own father had been heretic he would have carried faggots to the stake, Carafa devoted his pontificate almost entirely to the persecution of true and supposed dissenters. Cardinals Morone and Pole, a large number of bishops, and even such a candid soul as St. Filippo Neri were on his list of suspects. He also issued the most thorough and cruel measures against the Jews that the papacy had ever approved. His crowning work was the publication of the first complete *Index of Forbidden Books,* on 21 December 1558. When he died a few months later, the Roman people overthrew his statue, attacked the building of the Holy Office, and freed all the prisoners. But the blow had been struck; although some of Paul IV's suspected heretics were to make splendid careers in the Church, and some measures were soft-pedaled, there was no return to the half-frivolous, half-charitable indulgence of the Renaissance popes.

Whatever the merits of the Counter-Reformation, we may not make little of the fact that it displaced the prime mover of religious observance from love to fear; and since most people could not change their practices and beliefs at the nod of inquisitors, it promoted hypocrisy more effectively than had the tyranny of Renaissance princes. Ironically, the last influential Neoplatonic treatise that appeared on love as the way to God and the mover of the universe was the *Dialoghi d'amore* by Judah Abrabanel, alias Leone Ebreo, a Portuguese Jew who had lived in Italy the precarious but not unprotected life of his coreligionists after 1492. The book, published after his death (in 1535), was widely read and imitated by Italian writers, who pretended to believe that the author had been converted to Christianity.

One of the easygoing clergymen whom the new policy of the popes forced to pay tribute to morality and smoke out heresy, was Monsignor Della Casa, appointed inquisitor in Venice (1547). As such, he banned subversive books and prosecuted dissenters, without unrequired cruelty but with the servile diligence he was to recommend to inferiors in his second treatise. The job, however, may have interfered with his rest, if we are to believe the following sonnet:

> O Sleep, o peaceful son of the still Night,
> o darkness-drenchéd solace of diseased
> mankind, o sweet oblivion of the grief
> that weighs down life and makes it harsh with fight,
>
> succor at last my weary heart, and send
> it rest; relieve these limbs of mine, that are
> so frail and tir'd; o fly to me, good Sleep,
> and over me thy dusky wings extend.
>
> Where is now Silence, shy of day and shine?
> Where are soft Dreams, whose evanescent trace
> is swiftly wont to come right after thine?
>
> Alas! I call thee in vain, in vain I pray
> those icy shades. My quilt is made of stones,
> on it my cruel nights I waste away!

What makes the sonnet especially effective in expressing restlessness is an innovation which parallels those of manneristic architecture and painting: sentences do not fit snugly in the balanced framework of each line, as they did in Petrarch's classic models, but wind around a line and break capriciously in the midst of another. The subject of the sonnet, on the other hand, is a favorite theme of the declining Renaissance, even as spring, love, and hope were the leitmotifs of the early Renaissance. Night, sleep, death, repentance, almost obsessively recur in Michelangelo's bitter sonnets. Repentance and fear of death alter-

nate with spells of enraptured love in the mellow sonnets of Gaspara
Stampa. Luigi Tansillo, in two remarkable sonnets, relives the tragic
adventure of Icarus, who spurned life to shoot for the stars: no life, he
says, can equal the beauty of that death. There had been poems on
Icarus before, but none as poignant.

A pall of gloom envelops the last period of the Renaissance, even as a
flurry of hope had greeted the period of youth. Guicciardini had
recorded in his personal reflections a desolate longing: "Three things I
wish I could see before dying, but I doubt I shall see any of them, even
if I lived a long time: a well ordered republican life in our city, Italy
freed from all barbarians, and the world freed from the tyranny of
these wicked priests." He died in 1540, his wishes unfulfilled, and the
following years made them look even more unrealistic. In his *Courtier,*
Castiglione had deplored the Italian fad of imitating the dresses of
other nations, and while approving dark suits for ordinary occasions,
he recommended colorful ones for festivities. The increasing influence
of the Spanish conquerors, however, brought in its trail the fashion of
starkly black robes. We can watch it creeping in through Titian's
gallery of portraits: the early ones are still full of color, but his late
portrait of a Venetian ambassador, a symphony in black, matches the
Spanish gloom of his portraits of Emperor Charles V.

Must we share that gloom? Certainly the twilight of the Renaissance
did not immediately extinguish Italian creativity or destroy the estab-
lished economic and behavioral structures. For another fifty years Italy
was able to produce such people as Torquato Tasso, Gian Lorenzo
Bernini, Claudio Monteverdi, and Galileo Galilei, to mention only four
giants. At the same time, enduring peace and improving morality, even
at the cost of much humiliation and repression, had certain beneficial
effects. All the same, it is impossible to deny that Italy's stature at the
end of the Renaissance was smaller than at the beginning. The seven-
teenth century brought it further down and, worst of all, made the
Italians less aware of their slipping. But could any other nation have
remained longer on the peaks which Italy reached between 1453 and
1559? Had not Athens, long before, fallen from grace more steeply and
irreparably than did Florence, her younger rival? We do not have to
look for internal blemishes to explain the passing of a prodigy. True,
there were in Renaissance Italy too many wicked princes and sinful
prelates, but this was not peculiar to that country: think, for instance,
of Henry VIII and his court. There was callousness in regard to the

needs of country people, but Italy did not see a Martin Luther answer a revolt of peasants with a call for their extermination. There was no solidarity against foreign armies, but German Protestants and Turkish Muslims at that time allied with the French, and, later, French Catholics welcomed Spanish intervention. In short, most of the charges which contemporaries or later generations have leveled at Renaissance Italy would fit her neighbors as well; and it is not the historian's burden to evaluate the standards and transgressions of another age in the dubious light of the standards and transgressions of his own.

Like all other periods of history, the Italian Renaissance died because it had been born. As Leonardo put it, "the water you touch in a river is the last that has gone and the first that is coming." But this should not drive us to label the Renaissance "an age of transition," as some of its best knowers suggest; on the contrary, it had a most complex personality, all its own. Its image has been blurred, I am afraid, by its early worshipers as often as by its detractors. Retroactive religious or nationalistic moralism has unduly tarnished it, but the lingering claims of its first admirers have restored it beyond recognition. Nobody should believe any more that the Italian Renaissance "discovered the world and man," although it did make progress on the way. Man had been forever exploring his own conscience, and in this direction the Renaissance gained less than the Middle Ages or the Reformation; but its artists and scientists helped man to know his body, and this was no mean achievement. As for the world, the Eastern hemisphere had been rediscovered by Marco Polo and his contemporaries in the thirteenth century; Columbus, who showed the way to the Western hemisphere after the Scandinavians and the Vivaldi brothers, was one of the most medieval-minded men that haunted the Renaissance. Almost at the end of the period, Copernicus took the first, crucial step toward the discovery of the universe; but people had to wait for men like Giordano Bruno to assess the philosophical consequences of it, and Bruno died a victim of the Counter-Reformation. Again, it seems preposterous to ascribe to the Italian Renaissance a new spirit of liberty, when the liberty of the communes yielded to the tyranny of princes and foreign kings; a new awareness of law, when the school of Bologna was more than three centuries old; a new economic prosperity, when Italy was only striving to bring back the world of unlimited opportunity which had collapsed in the fourteenth century. And it detracts nothing from the glory of the Italian Renaissance to say that it did not create its rational cities and states but transformed them from a medieval work of business into a timeless work of art.

While paying to the glory of the Italian Renaissance the sincere tribute of a medievalist, I have so far avoided an expression which often recurs in Francesco De Sanctis' history of literature: *superficial,* which, of course, is not the same thing as *shallow.* The word may easily be misinterpreted, and it fails to convey the variety, riches, and earnestness of the civilization of the Renaissance in Italy. Yet there seems to be no term that can describe better a distinctive feature of that civilization, its tendency to spread in breadth still more than in depth. Both its astounding achievements and its forgivable failures were conditioned by the thinness of its framework; it was brilliant because fragile, and fragile because brilliant. All civilizations are given shape by a minority; but the elite of the Renaissance was not a cross section of the best or most fortunate exponents of the entire population. It was a self-appointed, exclusive group, whose tastes and beliefs were different from those of the vulgar people of whatever class. The standard-bearers strove to live in a world of beauty, unperturbed by winter, war, wrath, and common worries. Such a world was neither unreal nor unattainable, but it had to be balanced on a tightrope, forever shaken by the miseries of life. Leonardo, who tried all of its meanders, left unfinished three quarters of his work; Michelangelo consumed himself in the effort to grasp it; Pico hoped to rise on it by philosophical and cabalistic art; Ariosto invited the assistance of his winged horse; Machiavelli endeavored to unravel some of its tricks. More modestly, Pietro Bembo suggested that no one should walk the tightrope beyond his ability and upbraided Dante for having overreached himself: "How much more praise would he have deserved, if he had undertaken to write on a less high and less broad subject, and had kept it always in that moderate course, whereas by choosing such an extensive and magnificent subject, he often lapsed into writing most low and vile things. . . . His *Comedy* can be compared to a beautiful and spacious corn field, all infested by wild oats, darnel, and sterile weeds." [18]

Let us applaud the famous men of the Italian Renaissance, as they perform on the tightrope. And let us neither hiss nor cry when they fall.

Notes

Notes to I: Ancestry

1. R. L. Reynolds, *Europe Emerges* (Madison, Wis., 1961); F. C. Lane, "At the Roots of Republicanism," *American Historical Review,* LXXI (1966). See also A. Sapori, "Medioevo e Rinascimento," *Nuove questioni di storia medievale* (Milan, 1964).

2. I am quoting almost literally Panofsky's statement in the revised version of a lecture first delivered at the Metropolitan Museum of Art—"Artist, Scientist, Genius: Notes on the 'Renaissance-Dämmerung' "—and ultimately published in W. K. Ferguson *et al., The Renaissance, Six Essays* (New York, 1962), pp. 123ff. (henceforth quoted as *Metropolitan Symposium*). But Panofsky had already toyed with the idea in earlier papers, especially in the original version of his "Renaissance and Renascences," *Kenyon Review,* VI (1944). later revised and reprinted in E. Panofsky, *Renaissance and Renascences in Western Art* (Stockholm, 1960).

3. Naturally I do not imply that the Renaissance brought no change in the study and interpretation of Roman law. Legal thought never stands still. Its ceaseless evolution in Italy was mapped long ago, and recently a rash of studies on Roman law outside Italy has introduced a stronger term, revolution; see, for instance, J. H. Franklin, *Jean Bodin and the Sixteenth-Century Revolution in the Methodology of Law and History* (New York, 1963). I fail to see a "mutational change" in the substantial, but moderate, progress of Roman law at that time. Not without reason, Italian historians of law used to call the second half of the Middle Ages, not the Renaissance, the "age of the legal Renaissance"; and even that term lost favor when Francesco Calasso argued that nothing on earth can be born again if it has really died and compared the blossoming of Roman law in the Middle Ages to the simultaneous emergence of Romance languages and Romanesque art. For a brief account of the subject see R. S. Lopez, *The Birth of Europe* (New York, 1967), pp. 184ff.

4. That the civilization of the Italian Renaissance, as described in Burckhardt's classic work, was essentially the product of a self-appointed elite is, I believe, an almost undisputed fact; contra, but on shaky grounds, is L. Olschki, *The Genius of Italy* (New York, 1949). I fully agree with D. Hay, *The Italian Renaissance in Its Historical Background* (Cambridge, 1961), that the historical significance of what he aptly calls "the style of living" of the Renaissance is not a whit diminished by its failure to percolate to the masses. But I cannot agree that the difference was no greater than we must normally expect between educated and uneducated people. In the Middle Ages, the Italian urban elite was not estranged from the common folk; Aquinas and Dante may have talked above the head of their fellow citizens, but they reached for the same God. In

the Renaissance, Pico's intellectual God was not at all the same as that of his humbler contemporaries; with the latter, Pico shared a traditional God, to whom he turned in private and in the hour of death.

5. I might add that in my opinion the increasing stress that Renaissance historians have been placing during the latest fifty years on the philosophical background of Renaissance art, letters, and politics has gone as far as it safely can. No matter how important the ideological (and economic) underpinning, we must not lose sight of art, letters, and politics as self-propelled drives, which may have influenced philosophy as much as, or more than, they were influenced by it.

6. F. Chabod, *Machiavelli and the Renaissance* (Cambridge, Mass., 1958); later works can usually be tracked down with the help of such magazines as *Renaissance Quarterly* and *Bibliothèque d'Humanisme et Renaissance.* In the notes of the present little book I have usually limited my references to a few recent studies; these studies in turn have references, and Chabod's bibliography is ample enough. However, the shorter but excellent bibliography of A. Molho, ed., *Social and Economic Foundations of the Italian Renaissance* (New York, 1969), which I received when correcting proofs of this book, lists a few recent publications I had overlooked.

Notes to II: Youth

1. On economic matters I have written and am still writing a number of studies, to which I have to refer for a more detailed examination and bibliography of most of the problems mentioned here and in the rest of this little book. Two papers are specifically concerned with the economy of the Renaissance in Europe: "Hard Times and Investment in Culture," *Metropolitan Symposium;* "The Economic Depression of the Renaissance," in collaboration with H. A. Miskimin, *Economic History Review,* 2d ser., XIV (1962), followed by a debate with C. M. Cipolla in the same magazine, XVI (1964). A longer chronological span is covered in my chapter on the trade of southern Europe in the *Cambridge Economic History of Europe,* II (Cambridge, 1952; a revised edition is forthcoming) and in my book *The Commercial Revolution of Medieval Europe and the Beginning of the Modern World* (forthcoming, Englewood Cliffs, N.J., 1970).

2. I do not mean, of course, to deprecate the recent emphasis of economic historians of the prestatistical age on exploratory statistical work. A cautious quantitative approach has helped me ever since I wrote the second of my books, *Studi sull'economia genovese nel medio evo* (Turin, 1936), and the paper on "The Economic Depression of the Renaissance" is based on fragments of statistical evidence. Other figures have been assembled in G. Luzzatto, *Storia economica di Venezia dall'XI al XVI secolo* (Venice, 1961); J. Heers, *Gênes au XV⁰ siècle* (Paris, 1960); E. Fiumi, *Storia economica e sociale di San Gimignano* (Florence, 1961); J. Delumeau, *L'Alun de Rome* (Paris, 1963); D. Herlihy, *Medieval and Renaissance Pistoia* (New Haven, Conn., 1967); and C. Rotelli, *L'economia agraria di Chieri attraverso i catasti dei secoli XIV–XVI* (Milan, 1967), to mention only a few recent books. Nevertheless, we may not forget that all the

available figures are limited to short periods, or to single commodities, or to individual towns (often of moderate importance); that most of them are of dubious accuracy; and that, no matter how many fragments of Renaissance economic statistics may be recovered, the entire picture will always depend on debatable hypotheses and judgments of value.

3. The Genoese graph is discussed in greater detail in two papers of mine, "Quattrocento genovese," *Rivista Storica Italiana,* LXXV (1963), and "Market Expansion: The Case of Genoa," *Journal of Economic History,* XXIX (1964); see also the comments of F. C. Lane on the second paper (*ibid.*).

4. While describing the economic trend as I see it, admittedly on the basis of skimpy evidence, I wish to distinguish an area of virtually unanimous agreement among modern interpreters from a still debated ground. Hardly any economic historian today would question the general profile of the three phases of a secular fluctuation: a crest in the late thirteenth and early fourteenth centuries, a trough in the late fourteenth and early fifteenth, and a crest in the late fifteenth. What is debated is whether the second crest was substantially lower than the first or approximately as high (if not higher). The majority of historians, including Lopez and Miskimin, now believe that it was lower; a smaller but spirited group, including Cipolla, contend that it was approximately as high. Relatively neutral surveys of the conflict of opinions may be found in J. Heers, *L'Occident aux XIV* et XV* siècles: Aspects économiques et sociaux* (Paris, 1963), and in W. K. Ferguson, "Recent Trends in the Economic Historiography of the Renaissance," *Studies in the Renaissance,* VII (1960).

5. Harry Miskimin, my talented colleague and friend, has contributed his skill in drawing this graph (and the other graph, too), but I bear full responsibility for its shape. For the period before 1450 I have used the figures suggested in the thorough study of E. Fiumi, "Fioritura e decadenza dell'economia fiorentina," *Archivio Storico Italiano,* CXV–CXVII (1957–59). It is my impression that his estimates are slightly too low (that is, they underestimate the number of people who were not included in the censuses he uses), but consistent underestimation would not affect the profile. Fiumi does not offer figures after 1450 but merely states that henceforth the population grew at a sluggish pace. If we admit that his figure of 40,000 inhabitants for 1450 may be too low and that the figure of 50,000 inhabitants for 1529, offered by a sixteenth-century historian, Benedetto Varchi, may be slightly too high, we may integrate the profile more or less as I have it. No doubt the entire graph is to some extent hypothetical, but it is supported by bits of information from other writers.

6. See, for instance, E. Carpentier, *Une Ville devant la peste: Orvieto et la peste noire* (Paris, 1963); W. M. Bowsky, "The Impact of the Black Death upon Sienese Government and Society," *Speculum,* XXXIX (1964); A. Celli, *The History of Malaria in the Roman Campagna* (London, 1933); G. Cherubini, "Qualche considerazione sulle campagne dell'Italia centro-settentrionale tra l'XI e il XV secolo," *Rivista Storica Italiana,* LXXIX (1967), and, for a brilliant world-wide view of the early stages of the crisis, J. Glénisson, *Les Découvertes* (Paris, 1966). We still lack, however, a general survey of malaria; the later recurrences of the plague have not been studied as thoroughly as the first outbreak; research on climate and its variations is still in its infancy.

7. It must be noted, however, that while the objectives and scope of wars shrank after 1454, total peace was still the exception rather than the rule in the forty years that followed. On the other hand, the steep rise of taxation was to a

small extent compensated by a measure of rationalization in the fiscal system of each state. In general, taxation tended to shift emphasis from indirect to direct, and often progressive, levies on assessed property and income; methods of assessments also tended to improve; and so forth.

8. See, for instance, C. Klapisch-Zuber and J. Day, "Villages désertés en Italie," in *Villages désertés et histoire économique* (Paris, 1965); C. M. Cipolla, "L'economia milanese, 1350–1500," in *Storia di Milano*, VIII (Milan, 1962); F. C. Lane, several essays in his *Venice and History* (Baltimore, 1966); A. Sapori, several essays in his *Studi di storia economica* (3 vols., Florence, 1956–65); and T. O. De Negri, *Storia di Genova* (Milan, 1968). In English, besides the little book of G. Luzzatto, *An Economic History of Italy . . . to the Beginning of the Sixteenth Century* (London and New York, 1961), there are general surveys and bibliographies on various aspects of Quattrocento economy in several chapters of the *Cambridge Economic History of Europe*, 2d ed., I–III: P. Jones on agriculture (far better than G. Mickwitz on the same subject in the first edition, but some of Mickwitz' remarks are still useful); R. S. Lopez on trade; R. de Roover on business techniques; and C. M. Cipolla on economic policies.

9. Quotations from both Cotrugli and Uzzano come from R. S. Lopez and I. W. Raymond, *Medieval Trade in the Mediterranean World* (New York, 1955), pp. 413–18 and 420–21. Note that Cotrugli, a merchant from Ragusa (Dubrovnik) who became a minister of Ferdinand I of Sicily and Aragon, wrote his book allegedly in 1458; but it was printed only in 1573, probably with some alterations. See the old work of C. P. Kheil, *Benedetto Cotrugli: Ein Beitrag zur Geschichte der Buchhaltung* (Vienna, 1906), and the general comments and bibliography on commercial manuals in my paper, "Stars and Spices," forthcoming in *Robert L. Reynolds Memorial Essays*.

10. See Rucellai's *Zibaldone*, ed. A. Perosa (London, 1960), and, on him, the old book of G. Marcotti, *Un mercante fiorentino e la sua famiglia* (Florence, 1881). His attitude was far from untypical in Quattrocento Florence; see, for instance, R. de Roover, *The Rise and Decline of the Medici Bank* (Cambridge, Mass., 1963); L. Martines, *The Social World of the Florentine Humanists, 1390–1460* (Princeton, N.J., 1963); and A. Sapori, preface to *I libri degli Alberti del Giudice* (Milan, 1952). Comments and bibliography on the change of attitude of Genoese and Venetian merchants after 1350 can be found in Benjamin Kedar's dissertation (Yale University, 1969), now being prepared for publication. Note also Cotrugli's complaint that his fellow citizens and merchants in Ragusa "as they begin to increase their capital they begin to build or to overturn stones in making gardens, vineyards, and in other pursuits" instead of reinvesting it in gainful enterprises. For a general survey of merchants' attitudes in the Quattrocento one can still use Y. Renouard, *Les Hommes d'affaires italiens du moyen âge* (Paris, 1949); a shorter roundup is offered by J. Macek, "La Renaissance italienne," *Historica* (Prague), IX (1964).

11. In my opinion, the sociological generalizations of A. von Martin, *Sociology of the Renaissance* (Oxford, 1944), and A. Hauser, *The Social History of Art* (New York, 1960), in spite of their merits as handy collections of factual data, are rather misleading. They are based on obsolete assessments of the economic underpinning of Renaissance society and, above all, they fail to recognize the extreme diversity of the components of that peculiar elite, access to which did not depend on precise and uniform requisites of blood, income, education, or even legitimate birth. What we need is a patient canvasing of prosopography and

family history in each of the various Renaissance centers. A large amount of material was gathered by the older generations of historians and critics, from Burckhardt himself to Voigt, Gothein, and Rossi; research has become more systematic with such scholars as Baron, Garin, Vinay, Ferriguto, Trinkaus, Bruckner, Martines, Conti, and Molho (to mention only a few); but there still remains a great deal to be done.

12. The classic work of W. H. Woodward, *Studies in Education during the Age of the Renaissance* (Cambridge, 1906), is still valuable as far as it goes, but it does not go far enough. It misses almost entirely the connections between medieval and Renaissance education, and it systematically underplays the role of universities. These and other aspects of Renaissance education have recently been examined in full detail in one or another of the papers of P. O. Kristeller, collected under the titles *Studies in Renaissance Thought and Letters* (Rome, 1956) and *Renaissance Thought* (New York, 1961–65). I refer to them for the bibliography of the subject, adding only that E. Garin, *L'umanesimo italiano* (Bari, 1952) has a preface and an epilogue not included in the German translation quoted by Kristeller, and that D. J. Geanakoplos, *Greek Scholars in Venice* (Cambridge, Mass., 1962), contains fresh material on Greek studies, which I have been unable to discuss in the present book.

13. L. B. Alberti, *De Iciarchia,* in A. Bonucci, ed., *Opere volgari* (Florence, 1845), bk. II, pp. 72ff.; and see, for instance, C. Grayson, "The Humanism of Alberti," *Italian Studies*, XII (1957); G. Santinella, *Leon Battista Alberti, una visione estetica del mondo e della vita* (Florence, 1962), with bibliography. Do we need to add that Alberti was by no means a frivolous man, or that he both praised and practised the active and useful life as a family man, a citizen, and an artist?

14. Obviously I become no more than a fairly well read layman as I move from history proper to literature; my opinions, for whatever they may be worth, stem primarily from my subjective reactions to primary sources. But I have sought the help of several basic surveys and monographs, of which I shall mention here the most important ones. Like Burckhardt's *Civilization of the Renaissance in Italy,* Francesco De Sanctis' classic *History of Italian Literature* (English trans., New York, 1959), though marked by the mood of his time, still conveys a message of unsurpassed importance. I also found many pages of F. Flora, *Storia della letteratura italiana* (3d ed., Milan, 1945), and certain comments of A. Momigliano, *Antologia della letteratura italiana* (Messina, 1932), particularly suggestive. Above all I found precious, not only for the abundance of information and critical judgment but also for their almost exhaustive bibliographies, V. Rossi, *Il Quattrocento* (Milan, 1933), and the cooperative *Storia della letteratura italiana* under the editorship of E. Cecchi and N. Sapegno (Milan, 1966–), henceforth quoted as Cecchi and Sapegno. The latter is more recent, but not all of its essays are of top quality (though many are), and Rossi's monumental work is not really superseded.

15. On the relation between landscape and works of art there are interesting remarks in E. Sereni, *Storia del paesaggio agrario italiano* (Bari, 1961), and in E. H. Gombrich, "Renaissance Artistic Theory and the Development of Landscape Painting," *Gazette des Beaux-Arts* (May–June 1953). For comments and bibliography on the authors I mention see D. De Robertis, "L'esperienza poetica del Quattrocento," in Cecchi and Sapegno, III. The authorship of *Nencia da Barberino* is still debated; but even if the poem is eventually taken from Lorenzo

and ascribed to Giambullari or somebody else, we would reach approximately the same conclusions on Lorenzo's attitude in regard to the country and country people on the basis of the *Selve d'amore* and other poems which are certainly his. Let me note in passing that contemporary criticism often shows a tendency to reduce works of art to a cluster of *topoi* or clichés and literary symbols. The tendency is not unwarranted, but we must not overstress it. Granted that the roses of the Renaissance descend from those of Petrarch and Virgil, that does not mean that Renaissance poets never saw or smelled a rose.

16. Here I have taken advantage of the layman's right to express his personal preferences. Boiardo still has a few stanch supporters, who endeavor to place him almost as high as Ariosto; I find his epic poem vastly inferior not only to Ariosto's and Pulci's, but also to Boiardo's own lyric poems, which convey a faint echo of the elegance of Petrarch. On the other hand, I am not too impressed by the charge of vulgarity that the aristocratic tradition of Italian literature has leveled and still levels on Pulci. It seems to me that his learned coarseness is of the same kind, if not necessarily the same quality, as that of Rabelais, Ruzzante, and the *commedia dell'arte*. It exudes a powerful joy of life and creates convincing characters. Both in Italy and in the United States I have found it difficult to interest my students in Boiardo's inventions, but response to Margutte and Astarotte has been consistently warm. Note that the correct title of Pulci's poem is *Morgante,* although *Morgante Maggiore* has often been used. For bibliography see R. M. Ruggieri, *L'umanesimo cavalleresco italiano da Dante al Pulci* (Rome, 1962), and, in English, T. M. Greene, *The Descent from Heaven: A Study in Epic Continuity* (New Haven, Conn., 1963).

17. The most eloquent and erudite advocate of "civic virtue" as the leading political ideal of the Renaissance is H. Baron, especially in his *The Crisis of the Early Italian Renaissance* (Princeton, N.J., 1955), a good antidote against the old prejudice that made Renaissance politics an anteroom of Hell. An ideal that is shared by a large number of intellectual leaders and endorsed by a large number of governments must be regarded as a historical reality of the highest importance, even if it is not reflected in practice. Nevertheless, it would be naïve to overlook the other side of the coin and idealize. One could say, with some oversimplification, that in the age of the communes most intellectuals and governments praised religious virtue and practised civil virtue, whereas in the Renaissance they praised civil virtue and practised functional "virtù," that is, expediency. Much the same discrepancy prevails today, when we praise world unity and practise the balance of power; the ideal is highly significant, but we also have to take into account the performance.

18. Probably the best guide through the maze of Italian political history in the late Quattrocento is N. Valeri, *L'Italia nell'età dei principati, 1343–1516* (Verona, 1950). L. Simeoni, *Le signorie* (Milan, 1950), is more detailed but drab; E. R. Labande, *L'Italie de la Renaissance* (Paris, 1954), pays greater attention to the economic and social background of politics but is shorter; F. Ercole, *Dal comune al principato* (Florence, 1929), deals mainly with political theory and institutions. There is no dearth of good, recent books in English, but they generally devote more attention to political theory and cultural history than to political facts and deal with all of Europe rather than with Italy alone: see, for instance, D. Hay, *Europe in the Fourteenth and Fifteenth Centuries* (New York, 1966), which, like the earlier book by the same author, *The Italian Renaissance,* becomes more sketchy after 1450; M. P. Gilmore, *The World of Humanism, 1453–1517* (New York, 1952); W. K. Ferguson, *Europe in Transition, 1300–*

1520 (Boston, 1962); S. H. Thomson, *Europe in Renaissance and Reformation* (New York, 1963). Perhaps the largest storehouse of information is Will Durant's best seller, *The Renaissance* (New York, 1953); it reads well, but the information is not always accurate and the interpretation is often superficial.

19. The debate on moral problems is virtually coterminous with the broader discussion of the historical concept of the Renaissance. On this, it will be enough to refer to W. K. Ferguson, *The Renaissance in Historical Thought* (Boston, 1948), and, for a few more recent works, to the bibliography of Chabod, *Machiavelli and the Renaissance*. On the other hand, a matter-of-fact, unemotional, statistical canvasing of moral standards and performance is still an unsatisfied want. See, however, the excellent pioneer essay of N. Tamassia, *La famiglia italiana nei secoli decimoquinto e decimosesto* (Palermo, 1910), and other works on private life in various Italian towns, many of which are listed by G. Fasoli, "La vita quotidiana nel medioevo italiano," in *Nuove questioni di storia medioevale* (Milan, 1964).

20. Three short papers supply good introductions to the complex problem of the relation between traditional religiousness and the religious attitudes of the intellectuals: R. H. Bainton, "Man, God, and the Church," *Metropolitan Symposium;* P. O. Kristeller, "Paganism and Christianity" and "The Moral Thought of Renaissance Humanism," both reprinted in his *Renaissance Thought*. The most recent, detailed surveys of church history in the fifteenth century are volumes XIV and XV of A. Fliche and V. Martin, ed., *Histoire de l'église:* E. Delaruelle, E. R. Labande, and P. Ourliac, *L'Eglise au temps du Grand Schisme et de la crise conciliaire* (Paris, 1962–64), and R. Aubenas and R. Ricard, *L'Eglise et la Renaissance, 1449–1517* (Paris, 1951); they have excellent bibliographies.

21. On Latin humanism and the Roman tradition the bibliography is enormous; to save myself the embarrassment of choosing between many good works, of which the most important are not the most recent ones, I refer to the selected list of Chabod, *Machiavelli and the Renaissance*, pp. 225ff. On vernacular literature R. A. Hall, *The Italian Questione della lingua* (Chapel Hill, N.C., 1942), offers a good introduction and bibliography. P. O. Kristeller, "The Origin and Development of the Language of Italian Prose," in *Renaissance Thought,* puts forward interesting arguments for the parallel and unbroken development of both Latin and Italian; in my opinion, however, he tends to overstate his case. Granted that the vernacular never died as an informal written language and that Latin long preserved its function as the language of formal prose, it seems undeniable that in the early Quattrocento the vernacular lost ground. Among monographs, G. Folena, *La crisi linguistica del Quattrocento e l'Arcadia di I. Sannazaro* (Florence, 1952), is especially valuable. Concerning Pontano, whose poems we would recommend to the attention of all who can read Latin, see Arnaldi's remarks in F. Arnaldi, L. Gualdo Rosa, and L. Monti Sabia, *Poeti latini del Quattrocento* (Milan, 1964), and, in English, J. Sparrow, "Latin Verse of the High Renaissance," in E. F. Jacob, ed., *Italian Renaissance Studies* (London, 1960).

22. The letter "of Lorenzo" to Federigo of Aragon can be read in G. A. Brucker, *Renaissance Italy* (New York, 1958), pp. 38ff.; it was composed, however, by Poliziano, as M. Santoro, "Poliziano o il Magnifico?," *Giornale Italiano di Filologia,* I (1948), has proved. On Accolti, who was chancellor of the Florentine Republic, there is no full study, but we can use the short, perceptive characterization of E. Garin, "I cancellieri umanisti della repubblica fiorentina,"

reprinted in his *Scienza e vita civile nel Rinascimento italiano* (Bari, 1965), a two-page profile in Martines, *Social World,* and several incidental remarks in Rossi, *Quattrocento.* It is worth noting that Accolti did not buttress praise of his own time with disparagement of the Middle Ages, witness his poem "De bello a Christianis contra barbaros gesto," a story of the First Crusade.

23. E. Garin, *Giovanni Pico della Mirandola: Vita e dottrina* (Florence, 1937), and P. O. Kristeller, *The Philosophy of Marsilio Ficino* (New York, 1943), are the best introductions to the two major philosophical figures. Two broader panoramas, observed from very different, debatable points of view, are found in G. Toffanin, *A History of Humanism* (New York, 1954), and E. Cassirer, *The Individual and the Cosmos in Renaissance Philosophy* (Oxford, 1963). For the impact of Renaissance philosophy on art see E. Panofsky, *Studies in Iconology* (New York, 1939), and A. Chastel, *Marsile Ficin et l'art* (Geneva, 1954). On astrology L. Thorndyke, *History of Magic and Experimental Science,* III and IV (New York, 1934), still is the largest storehouse of information; see also A. J. Festugière, *La Révélation d'Hermes Trismegiste* (Paris, 1950). Much is made of the fact that Pico did not believe in astrology; but most people did, and perhaps we should not call superstition a belief that we now know was wrong, but was then rationally grounded in the religious and scientific doctrines of the time. As for the meanings and comparative influence of "virtù" and "fortuna," on which rivers of ink have been spilled, my impression is that no generalization is warranted. The dispute antedated the Renaissance; there were shifts in emphasis from one to another possible meaning of virtue and from one to another possible influence of fortune, but most Renaissance writers played with all the meanings and influences at the same time, because their judgment was simultaneously affected by their personality and experience as well as by rhetoric and philosophy.

24. The painstaking essay of Ida Maier, *Ange Politien* (Geneva, 1966), lists and exploits virtually everything that has written by and on that poet. On the other lyric poets of his age the latest study is D. De Robertis, "L'esperienza poetica del Quattrocento," in Cecchi and Sapegno. The best recent biography of Lorenzo il Magnifico is R. Palmarocchi, *Lorenzo de'Medici* (Turin, 1941). On the general historical background see W. Welliver, *L'impero fiorentino* (Florence, 1957), or, in English, C. M. Ady, *Lorenzo de'Medici and Renaissance Italy* (London, 1955).

25. The voluminous bibliography of the debated problem of the relation between popular and learned literature is quoted in the spirited essay of G. B. Bronzini, *Il mito della poesia popolare* (Rome, 1966). On literacy and related problems see C. M. Cipolla, *Literacy and Development in the West* (Harmondsworth, Middlesex, 1969), a stimulating book on a problem that needs further study. If his conclusions based on the notarial acts of 1450–59 Venice are correct, one is led to suggest that literacy may have followed the same trend as demography and economics, with a depression between 1350 and 1450 and a partial recovery in the late Quattrocento; for all we know about literacy in the early Trecento would indicate a lower proportion of illiterates. Similar conclusions are tentatively suggested, on other grounds, by H. Miskimin, *The Economy of Early Renaissance Europe, 1300–1460* (Englewood Cliffs, N.J., 1969).

26. The old book of R. de La Sizeranne, *Les Masques et les visages à Florence et au Louvre* (Paris, 1913), evokes the three Florentine beauties with flair, if

with excessive romanticism; it is pointedly ignored by Ida Maier, *Politien,* where all other significant writings and paintings concerning Simonetta and Albiera (but not Giovanna) are discussed at length. Among other recent writers who, while paying full attention to classic reminiscences and philosophical symbols underlying the works of art, do not forget their immediate physical models, I shall mention J. Lipman, "The Florentine Profile Portrait," *Art Bulletin,* XVIII (1936); E. H. Gombrich, "Botticelli's Mythologies," *Journal of the Warburg and Courtauld Institutes,* VIII (1945), and G. Creighton, "On Subject and Non-subject in Italian Renaissance Picture," *Art Bulletin,* XXXIV (1952). On poor Cassandra I know only an old study by C. Cavazzani, "Cassandra Fedele," *Archivio Veneto,* II (1907). On the theme of the Dance of Death see A. Tenenti, *Il senso della morte e l'amore della vita nel Rinascimento* (Turin, 1957).

27. At this point I had better disclaim any professional competence in the field of art history and claim only the privileges of a layman who endeavors, rightly or wrongly, to detect traces of the prevalent mood of an age in a few, arbitrarily chosen works of art. I like to look at these works and to read about them, but I realize that it is too late for me to become an expert; hence I shall not attempt to discuss technical points or to offer bibliographic advice. To fellow laymen, however, I would suggest further reading in the following recent, or fairly recent, general works: E. Battisti, *Rinascimento e Barocco* (Turin, 1960); A. Blunt, *Artistic Theory in Italy, 1450–1600* (Oxford, 1940); A. Chastel, *Art et religion dans la Renaissance italienne* (Paris, 1945); G. Chierici, *Il palazzo italiano dal secolo XI al XIX* (2d ed., Milan, 1964); K. Clark, *Landscape in Art* (London, 1949) and *The Nude* (1959); G. Dorfles, *Il divenire delle arti* (Turin, 1959); P. Francastel, *Peinture et société* (Lyons, 1951); E. H. Gombrich, *The Story of Art* (New York, 1956); P. Lavedan, *Histoire de l'art,* II (Paris, 1950); W. Paatz, *Die Kunst der Renaissance in Italien* (Stuttgart, 1954); N. Pevsner, *An Outline of European Architecture* (London, 1943); M. Pittaluga, *Arte italiana,* II and III (13th ed., Florence, 1957); J. Pope-Hennessy, *Italian Renaissance Sculpture* (New York, 1958); L. Venturi, *Italian Painting, Renaissance* and *Fifteenth Century* (Geneva, 1950–55); and R. Wittkower, *Architectural Principles in the Age of Humanism* (2d ed., London, 1952). I add an older, classic work, which surprisingly was translated into English only a few years ago, H. Wölfflin, *Renaissance and Baroque* (London, 1964).

28. The development of equestrian monuments has been recently reconstructed in a stimulating paper of H. W. Janson, "The Equestrian Monument from Cangrande della Scala to Peter the Great," in A. R. Lewis, ed., *Aspects of the Renaissance* (Austin, Tex., 1967). Note that Trivulzio's monument never went beyond the stage of preparatory sketches.

29. Filarete's comments and other relevant texts, in English translation, are easily available in E. G. Holt, *A Documentary History of Art* (2d ed., New York, 1957). The bibliography of the subject is very abundant; see, for instance, P. Lavedan, *Histoire de l'urbanisme,* II (2d ed., Paris, 1959); E. Garin, "La città ideale," in his *Scienza e vita civile;* and M. Morini, *Atlante di storia dell'urbanistica* (Milan, 1963). We are here in the borderland between art history and economic history, and I hope to deal with the subject in a work on the domestic architecture of the medieval town.

Notes to III: Maturity

1. Virtually all the relevant sources can be found in the monumental *Raccolta di documenti e studi pubblicati dalla Commissione Colombiana* issued on the occasion of the 1892 centennial; a few additional data are included in P. Revelli, *Elenco illustrativo della Mostra Colombiana Internazionale* (Genoa, 1950). On the Italian reaction to the discovery see R. Romeo, *Le scoperte americane nella coscienza italiana* (Naples, 1954); but the reaction was slow, and it is worth noting that the popes did not find it necessary to give the Church a definitive organization in America before 1511. On the other hand, a number of Italians, chiefly Genoese, took part in the early economic exploitation of the new land; see, for instance, R. Pike, *Enterprise and Adventure: The Genoese in Seville and the Opening of the New World* (New York, 1966), and C. Verlinden, "Le influenze italiane nella colonizzazione iberica," *Nuova Rivista Storica,* XXXVI (1952), one of many papers of that scholar on the subject.

2. The short, recent book of J. H. Parry, *The Age of Reconnaissance* (New York, 1963), is a far better introduction than B. Penrose's mediocre *Travel and Discovery in the Renaissance* (Cambridge, Mass., 1952). Without trying to sample the enormous bibliography of discovery, I would record my surprise at the extravagant praise usually lavished on S. E. Morison, *Admiral of the Ocean Sea* (Boston, 1942). No doubt it is better written than P. Revelli, *Cristoforo Colombo e la scuola cartografica genovese* (Rome, 1930), and more detailed than C. de Lollis, *Cristoforo Colombo nella leggenda e nella storia* (3d ed., Rome, 1923), but it offers a one-sided portrait of the man and ignores much of the background. On the latter E. Pandiani, *La vita della repubblica di Genova nell'età di Cristoforo Colombo* (Genoa, 1952), is helpful but of limited scope. In my opinion, a satisfactory study of Columbus and his time is still wanting.

3. F. Catalano, "Dall'equilibrio alla crisi italiana del Rinascimento," in N. Valeri, ed., *Storia d'Italia,* II (2d ed., Turin, 1964), is the most recent guide through the meanders of Italian politics and war up to 1500; it has a number of interesting comments but does not supersede the earlier works of Valeri and Simeoni on the same period. The essay that follows it in the same cooperative work (henceforth quoted as *Storia d'Italia*) — G. Sasso, "L'Italia del Machiavelli e l'Italia del Guicciardini" — is more forcefully organized and has a more helpful bibliographic note.

4. Isabella's comment, and a sonnet of Antonio Tebaldeo ("poor, but historically remarkable") with a similar remark, are quoted in Rossi, *Quattrocento.* The same comment, more fully developed, reappears in Machiavelli's *Prince.* Obviously it was a commonplace, but the princes did not take it to heart. Sasso aptly cites the following words of Lodovico il Moro, as recorded by a Venetian ambassador: "I confess that I have caused great harm in Italy, but I did it unwillingly, in order to maintain myself in the position where I am."

5. A. Castiglioni, *Il poema "Morbus gallicus"* (Turin, 1930) and *The Renaissance of Medicine in Italy* (Baltimore, 1934), will introduce the reader to Fracastoro, the physician and the classicist; but these are only two facets of his personality. *La Venexiana,* ed. and trans. by M. Valenti Pfeiffer (New York, 1950), a sensuous play intermingling Venetian dialect, Italian, and Bergamo

dialect, which is now usually ascribed to Verona-born Fracastoro, shows an entirely different angle; and there are still others. In general, on Fracastoro the writer the latest comments are in E. Bonora, "Il classicismo dal Bembo al Guarini," in Cecchi and Sapegno, IV; the essay is altogether better than G. Toffanin, *Il Cinquecento* (Rome, 1928), which is the sequel to Rossi's *Quattrocento* but is far less reliable, though somewhat more imaginative. On the impact of the disease there is a recent paper by H. Brabant, "L'Homme malade dans la société de la Renaissance," in *Individu et société à la Renaissance (Université Libre de Bruxelles, Travaux de l'Institut pour l'Etude de la Renaissance;* Brussels, 1967).

6. The dry, but extremely well-informed survey of A. Milano, *Storia degli ebrei in Italia* (Turin, 1963), tells the facts and gives the bibliography. On Daniel Norsa see further details in P. Norsa, "Una famiglia di banchieri, 1350–1950," *Bollettino dell'Archivio Storico del Banco di Napoli,* nos. 6 and 13 (1953, 1959). The "suspicion" of de La Sizeranne, *Masques et Visages,* p. 192, that St. Longinus in Mantegna's painting may be a sly portrait of Daniel Norsa, should become a certitude, in my opinion, considering its resemblance to Norsa's caricature in the anonymous painting. The latter is labeled with the inscription: "Debellata Hebraeorum temeritate." The beatification of Simon of Trent was revoked in 1965.

7. See, for instance, S. A. Nulli, *I processi delle streghe* (Turin, 1939); H. Haydn, *The Counter-Renaissance* (New York, 1950); and E. Battisti, *L'antirinascimento* (Florence, 1965). Granted that a methodical study of witchcraft in Renaissance Italy, which is still lacking, would probably disclose significant inroads of the sorcery psychosis, there are good reasons to believe that Italy was relatively spared by what G. Sarton called one of the two "new diseases" of the period, the other being, of course, syphilis ("The Quest for Truth," in *Metropolitan Symposium*). It is significant that witchcraft provides comic relief in the Italian theatre of the Renaissance, and no less significant that Jean Bodin (the famous writer, who did not extend his tolerant attitude to witches) charges the Italians, not without reason, with being unduly skeptical in regard to sorcery. See also G. Cocchiara, *Storia del folklore in Europa* (Turin, 1952). Of another book, G. Bonomo, *Caccia alle streghe* (Palermo, 1959), I have seen only the title.

8. On Florence in the twilight of the Quattrocento and the early Cinquecento see, for instance, F. Ercole, *Da Carlo VIII a Carlo V* (Florence, 1932); R. von Albertini, *Das florentinische Staatsbewusstsein im Uebergang von der Republik zum Prinzipat* (Berne, 1955); and the papers of L. Marks, "The Financial Oligarchy in Florence under Lorenzo," and N. Rubinstein, "Politics and Constitution in Florence at the End of the Fifteenth Century," in Jacob, *Italian Renaissance Studies.* Savonarola has been a pet subject for biographers, among whose divergent views I am not prepared to choose.

9. No doubt the condition of Italy was not always and everywhere as wretched as it would appear from this often cited report (*State Papers,* VII, 1849, Henry the Eighth, 226); but the frequency and duration of crises must have destroyed the delicate balance and moderate economic recovery of the late Quattrocento. In his introduction to a collection of essays, *Storia dell'economia italiana,* I (Turin, 1959), 17, C. M. Cipolla, who is more optimistic than I am on the Quattrocento recovery, describes the early Cinquecento with unmitigated gloom: "Wars, invasions, plagues, famines, destruction and economic depression dominate the scene. A few isolated areas are spared and draw profit from the general

turmoil . . . but the general picture is one of destitution and ruin." See also C. Barbagallo, "La crisi economico-sociale dell'Italia della Rinascenza," *Nuova Rivista Storica*, XXV (1950).

10. The most comprehensive discussion of the general problems of Italian politics, war, and society in the early Cinquecento is that of P. Pieri, *Il Rinascimento e la crisi militare italiana* (Turin, 1952). On the hard facts of political and military history the older works of E. Fueter, *Geschichte des Europäischen Staatensystems, 1492–1559* (Munich, 1919), and C. Barbagallo, *Storia universale*, IV (Milan, 1945), are partly superseded by the essay of Sasso and the books of Valeri and Simeoni already quoted. These, in turn, list some of the monographs on particular states and episodes. G. Mattingly's excellent *Renaissance Diplomacy* (New York, 1955) can be supplemented, for Venice, by W. Andreas, *Staatskunst und Diplomatie der Venezianer im Spiegel ihrer Gesandtenberichte* (Leipzig, 1943), and, on lack of union against the Turks, by some hints in my old paper, "Il principio della guerra veneto-turca nel 1463," *Archivio Veneto*, XV (1934).

11. On the whole I follow Chabod, *Machiavelli and the Renaissance*, which seems to me the best study on Machiavelli from the angle of Italian political problems. I should like to suggest further reading, but it is hard to pick a few works only from nearly one thousand titles singled out for special mention in the recent bibliography of D. Cantimori and L. Blasucci, "Niccolò Machiavelli," in Cecchi and Sapegno, IV, to say nothing of the new crop which the 1969 centennial is bringing out. For a large batch of recent contributions see the good critical roundup of E. Cochrane, "Machiavelli, 1940–60," *Journal of Modern History*, XXXIII (1961).

12. Machiavelli, *Discourses*, I, 12; *Art of War*, VII; similar ideas are expressed at other places in his works. But one can also find statements that seem to disagree with them, not only because Machiavelli fluctuates between expediency and idealism, but also because he is affected by the ever-changing political scene where he is an actor as well as an observer.

13. The direct quotation is from bk. I, 43. M. Rossi, *Baldassar Castiglione, la sua personalità, la sua prosa* (Bari, 1946), and E. Loos, *Baldassar Castiglione, Studien zur Tugendauffassung des Cinquecento* (Frankfurt a. M., 1955), supply good, recent introductions to a writer who has been in turn excessively praised and mercilessly ridiculed. Briefer statements on the opposite sides may be found in the introductions by M. Luzi and by G. Prezzolini to their editions of *The Courtier* (Milan, 1941; Milan, 1937). In English there is an old work by J. Cartwright, *Baldassar Castiglione: The Perfect Courtier, His Life and Letters* (London, 1908).

14. As I am getting to the greatest figures of the Renaissance, it becomes obvious that short bibliographic suggestions will be inadequate and long ones pretentious. Once more I shall refer to an essay in Cecchi and Sapegno, IV—in this instance a very perceptive one, L. Caretti's "Ludovico Ariosto"—and, for those who might want a longer bibliography than Caretti's, to G. Fatini, *Bibliografia della critica ariostea* (Florence, 1958). In addition I shall mention two essays that I have read recently: J. Huizinga, "Renaissance and Realism," in his *Men and Ideas* (New York, 1959), whose brilliant description of Ariosto's imaginative realism supplements the classic comments of De Sanctis and Benedetto Croce, and A. B. Giamatti, *The Earthly Paradise and the Renaissance Epic*

(Princeton, N.J., 1966), whose interpretation I found stimulating even where I was not fully convinced.

15. To my knowledge, the resemblance has not been noticed so far; but it seems obvious to me. No doubt the physical type attracted the artists of the time; the so-called *Madonna Benois* is one of Leonardo's earliest paintings, but it was repeated many times and by good painters, including even Raphael (the latter's copy of the Madonna, however, is lost.)

16. Although English use has the spelling *Mona,* the correct spelling is *Monna,* short for *Madonna,* lady.

17. If Leonardo's Leda has vanished, Correggio's has lost her head, which was badly repainted at a much later time; but the swan knows what he is doing. As for the so-called *Antiope,* an illustration of the Hypnerotomachia Poliphili representing Venus with a satyr has been identified as Correggio's source. But the source (late Quattrocento) is frigid and Correggio is not.

18. There is no recent monograph on Vittoria Colonna. In Italian, see especially Toffanin, *Cinquecento.* In English, there is the old book of M. F. Jerrold, *Vittoria Colonna, with Some Account of Her Friends and Her Times* (London, 1906). As for Lucrezia Borgia, I am afraid we cannot dismiss most of the charges listed somewhat brutally in G. Portigliotti, *The Borgia* (New York, 1928).

19. I am well aware, of course, that the earliest description of the painting (1530) calls it "the hamlet, on cloth, with the tempest, the gipsy girl, and the soldier"; also, that in Giorgione's first draft, as revealed by X rays, the "gipsy" was omitted, and a naked woman (perhaps the same woman who was eventually portrayed as the "gipsy"?) was in the place of the "soldier"; also, that the lightning and heavy clouds do not seem to produce any wind, so that we have a peculiarly quiet tempest. While attracted by the suggestion of L. Venturi, *Giorgione* (Rome, 1954), that the painting may have owed nothing to iconological or literary tradition, I see no necessity to deny that one or another of the mutually exclusive iconological hypotheses that have been put forward may actually be correct. What matters is that the physical models of the painting were people and scenes which in all probability Giorgione and his friend, Gabriele Vendramin, had actually seen. For bibliography see P. Zampetti's *Catalogo della mostra Giorgione e i Giorgioneschi* (Venice, 1955); a few later titles can be found in Battisti, *Rinascimento e Barocco.*

20. Excerpts from Leonardo's so-called *Paragone* (the title is modern) have been reprinted in Holt, *Documentary History;* the text of Michelangelo can be found in L. Venturi, *Theory and History of the Critic of Art* (New York, 1936), or, better, in the revised edition of that book, *Storia della critica d'arte* (Turin, 1964). In general, on the running discussion among Renaissance artists see J. A. Richter, *Paragone* (Oxford, 1949), and J. White, "Paragone: Aspects of the Relationship between Sculpture and Painting," in C. S. Singleton, ed., *Art, Science, and History in the Renaissance* (Baltimore, 1967). According to Vasari, Michelangelo was no less critical of what he called Titian's inadequacy of design. See also R. W. Lee, *Ut Pictura Poesis* (2d ed., New York, 1967).

21. See C. Trinkaus, *Adversity's Noblemen: The Italian Humanists on Happiness* (New York, 1940), and my paper, "Hard Times and Investment in Culture"; but the subject calls for more detailed research into the earnings and

income of artists and literary writers, some of whom had financial resources of their own.

22. The perspective of the Italian elite is well illustrated by a passage of Fracastoro (in his poem on syphilis, published in 1530 but written in 1521), which I quote in M. Gilmore's excellent translation: "Although a cruel tempest rages and the conjunction of the stars has been wicked, yet not wholly has the clemency of the gods been removed from us. If this century has seen a new disease, the ravages of war, the sack of cities, floods and drouth, yet it has also been able to navigate oceans denied to antiquity, and has reached . . . a whole world different from ours . . . . Our age also has seen a famous poet [Sannazzaro] whom even the sacred shade of Vergil has applauded; it has seen Bembo and, above all . . . the rule of Leo X who has brought back to Latium the rule of justice and law and who shelters all the arts" (*The World of Humanism*, p. 267). Not a word about Luther!

23. See J. H. Randall's introduction to Pomponazzi in E. Cassirer, P. O. Kristeller, and J. H. Randall, *The Renaissance Philosophy of Man* (Chicago, 1948), and its bibliography; also P. O. Kristeller, *Eight Philosophers of the Italian Renaissance* (Stanford, Cal., 1964), and, on a related problem, F. Gilbert, "Cristianesimo, umanesimo, e la bolla Apostolici Regiminis del 1513," *Rivista Storica Italiana*, LXXIX (1967).

24. The little poem describes an allegory often depicted by painters; see, for instance, the allegory of Occasion, Regret (?), and a man restrained by the latter as he tries to grasp the former, painted on a chimney piece in the Palazzo Ducale of Mantua (perhaps after a design of Mantegna.)

Notes to IV: Decline

1. Traditionally the political and military history of Italy from the beginning of the invasions to the final triumph of Spain is treated as a single unit. Hence the basic works of Sasso, Pieri, Simeoni, Fueter, Ercole, and others whom we have quoted for the "age of maturity" also serve as guides to the facts and bibliography of the "age of decline." The difference between the two ages is more forcefully pointed out in a series of studies by F. Chabod, ostensibly limited to the history of Milan, but actually covering the whole history of Italy and its relations with foreign powers. The earliest is entitled *Lo stato di Milano nell'impero di Carlo V* (Rome, 1934), and the latest, interrupted by the death of the author, is included in *Storia di Milano, IX* (Milan, 1961); the whole design is unraveled in the valuable critical study of G. Galasso, "Carlo V e Milano nell'opera di Federico Chabod," *Rivista Storica Italiana*, LXXII (1960).

2. See K. Helleiner's excellent chapter on population trends in the *Cambridge Economic History of Europe*, IV. To its bibliography one may add A. Bellettini, *La popolazione di Bologna dal secolo XV all'unificazione italiana* (Bologna, 1961); A. I. Pini, "Problemi demografici bolognesi del Duecento," *Atti e*

Memorie della Deputazione di Storia Patria per la Romagna, n.s., XVI–XVII (1969).

3. The only general survey of Italian economy in the Cinquecento—G. Luzzatto, *Storia economica dell'età moderna e contemporanea,* I (Padua, 1950)—is very useful, but brief and in some parts outdated. F. Mauro, *Le XVIe siècle, aspects économiques* (Paris, 1966) is more recent, but still sketchier on Italy. There are short accounts of specific sectors, such as A. Fanfani, *Storia del lavoro in Italia dalla fine del secolo XV* (Milan, 1943), and A. De Maddalena, "Il mondo rurale italiano nel Cinque e Seicento," *Rivista Storica Italiana,* LXXVI (1964), but most of the ground has never been covered. So long as preparatory monographs are too few to support a fresh synthesis, we must depend on two brilliant generalizations based on inadequate proofs: F. Braudel's monumental *La Méditerranée et le monde méditerranéen à l'époque de Philippe II* (2d rev. ed., Paris, 1966), and C. M. Cipolla's concise but dense "The Decline of Italy," *Economic History Review,* 2d ser., V (1952), revised and reprinted in Italian in his *Storia dell'economia italiana.* Some bibliographic help is supplied by M. R. Caroselli, "Saggio d'una bibliografia di storia economica italiana," *Economia e Storia,* V (1958).

4. M. Berengo, *Nobili e mercanti nella Lucca del Cinquecento* (Turin, 1965), is an excellent monograph; unfortunately, there is nothing of a comparable caliber for the other parts of Tuscany after the fall of the Florentine republic. For the time being, we can use the intelligent, but hasty book of R. Caggese, *Firenze dalla decadenza di Roma al risorgimento d'Italia,* I (Florence, 1913); some perceptive but, in my opinion, overoptimistic remarks are to be found in E. Cochrane, "The End of the Renaissance in Florence," *Bibliothèque d'Humanisme et Renaissance,* XXVII (1965). On the papal states, J. Delumeau, *Vie économique et sociale de Rome dans la seconde moitié du XVIe siècle* (Paris, 1962), is helpful for the earlier period also. There are two good books on the Neapolitan kingdom: G. Coniglio, *Il regno di Napoli al tempo di Carlo V* (Naples, 1951), and F. Caracciolo, *Il regno di Napoli nei secoli XVI e XVII,* I (Rome, 1966). See also G. Galasso, "La feudalità nel secolo XVI," reprinted in his *Dal comune all'unità, linee di storia meridionale* (Bari, 1969).

5. The abundant bibliography on Venice is quoted in the remarkable synthesis of Luzzatto, *Storia economica di Venezia,* and in the collected essays of Lane, *Venice and History.* That on Genoa is quoted in Lopez, "Market Expansion," and in De Negri, *Storia di Genova.* That on Milan is quoted in *Storia di Milano,* IX, and in A. Bosisio, *Storia di Milano* (Milan, 1960). In each case, except Venice (synthetically treated by Luzzatto), we have only works dealing with particular aspects, and a selective list would take an excessive amount of space, especially if we include studies on minor cities and regions, some of which have considerable importance. I shall only mention a valuable recent study of E. Grendi, "Traffico portuale, naviglio e consolati genovesi," *Rivista Storica Italiana,* LXXX (1968).

6. A middleman of literature more than a great artistic personality, Bembo has inspired no large-scale biography. See, however, B. Croce, "Il Bembo," in his *Poeti e scrittori del pieno e tardo Rinascimento,* III (Bari, 1952), and Toffanin's chapter on Bembo in his *Cinquecento.* For the general background see L. Baldacci, *Il petrarchismo italiano nel Cinquecento* (Milan, 1957), with bibliography. On the "questione della lingua," see Hall, *Italian Questione;* further

bibliographic data and a good discussion of the subject are found in Bonora, "Classicismo dal Bembo."

7. The brief, penetrating survey of L. Firpo, "Il pensiero politico del Rinascimento e della Controriforma," in *Questioni di storia moderna* (Milan, 1948), provides a good panorama of political thought and quotes the essential bibliography. Older surveys are those of C. Curcio, *Dal Rinascimento alla Controriforma* (Rome, 1934), and the pioneer work of G. Ferrari, *Corso sugli scrittori politici italiani* (Milan, 1861). Venice, of course, had had a few admirers even before the crisis of the Cinquecento. See, for instance, the praise of the Venetian nobility, as opposed to the Neapolitan nobility, in the dialogues of Cristoforo Landino, a Florentine contemporary of Alberti, quoted in Garin, *Umanesimo italiano*, p. 115.

8. The latest work is that of F. Gilbert, *Machiavelli and Guicciardini: Politics and History in Sixteenth Century Florence* (Princeton, N.J., 1965); its bibliography will serve as a guide for further study of the debate.

9. See, for instance, V. Luciani, *Francesco Guicciardini e la fortuna dell'opera sua* (Florence, 1949); V. de Caprariis, *Francesco Guicciardini dalla politica alla storia* (Bari, 1950); R. Ridolfi, *Vita di Francesco Guicciardini* (Rome, 1960).

10. *Galateo*, I; *Trattato degli uffici communi*, III. Not much has been written on Della Casa since the long essay of L. Campana, "Monsignor Della Casa e i suoi tempi," *Studi Storica*, XVI–XVIII (1907–9). While the introduction of P. Pancrazi to his edition of *Galateo* (Florence, 1940), is highly perceptive, that of G. Prezzolini to his edition of B. Castiglione and G. Della Casa, *Opere* (Milan, 1937), borders on libel. In English there is a short paper by W. L. Bullock, "The Lyric Innovations of Della Casa," *PMLA*, XLI (1926). I found the comments and bibliography of Bonora (himself a prominent Della Casa scholar), "Classicismo dal Bembo," most valuable.

11. Gaspara's profession is still debated in spite of the publication by A. Salza of compromising documents. B. Croce, in *Conversazioni critiche*, II (Bari, 1924), accepts the thesis that she was a courtesan; G. A. Cesareo, *Gaspara Stampa donna e poetessa* (Naples, 1920), defends her honor; E. Donadoni, *Gaspara Stampa* (Messina, 1919), cannot make up his mind. Does it really matter?

12. I have already supplied a random list of helpful books on Renaissance art, including so-called Mannerism. The select bibliography of L. Murray, *The Late Renaissance and Mannerism* (New York, 1967) contains a useful list of monographs on individual artists (mostly in English).

13. Again, as in the case of Giorgione's *Tempest,* I am fully aware that there are persuasive, if sometimes contradictory, allegorical explanations for the three paintings. Moreover, some of the people in them have been identified as true portraits of well-known men and women. Still I hope it is legitimate to draw inferences from the painter's choice of a specific model and a specific expression. F. Valcanover's critical comments in *L'opera completa di Tiziano* (Milan, 1969) are extremely valuable.

14. A. Mortier, *Ruzzante un dramaturge populaire de la Renaissance italienne,* II, *Oeuvres complètes* (Paris, 1926), 631 and 634. On Ruzzante and the beginnings of the *commedia dell'arte* see, for instance, S. D'Amico, *Storia del teatro drammatico,* II (Milan, 1950), and K. M. Lea, *Italian Popular Comedy* (Oxford, 1934).

15. See, for instance, O. Ore, *Cardano, the Gambling Scholar* (Princeton, N.J., 1953). On the debated question of the role of science in the Renaissance see, for instance, the papers of Sarton and Panofsky in *Metropolitan Symposium*. The debate, in my opinion, could easily be settled if we distinguished rationalism and realism, which were well developed at the beginning of the period and to some extent go back to the late Middle Ages, from science proper, which underwent no revolutionary change before the Cinquecento. In general, for the nonscientist, A. C. Crombie, *Medieval and Early Modern Science* (New York, 1959), is an excellent introduction; I have no ambition to offer bibliographic help in a field where I am still more of a layman than in literature and art.

16. The recent essay of V. de Caprariis, "L'Italia nell'età della Controriforma," in *Storia d'Italia*, II, seems to me the best survey of the religious problem. It certainly is far better than L. Cristiani's superficial *L'Eglise à l'époque du Concile de Trente* (Paris, 1948). F. C. Church, *The Italian Reformers* (New York, 1932); H. Jedin, *A History of the Council of Trent* (London, 1952–61); and D. Cantimori, *Eretici italiani del Cinquecento*, (Florence, 1939), and his collected *Studi di storia* (Turin, 1959), are also fundamental.

17. See, for instance, F. Chabod, "Per la storia religiosa dello Stato di Milano durante il dominio di Carlo V," *Annuario dell'Istituto Storico Italiano per l'età moderna* (Rome, 1938); R. Bainton, *Bernardino Ochino, esule e riformatore* (Florence, 1940); E. M. Wilbur, *A History of Unitarianism*, I (Cambridge, Mass., 1945); H. Jedin, *Gerolamo Seripando* (St. Louis, 1947); R. M. Douglas, *Jacopo Sadoleto* (Cambridge, Mass., 1959); B. M. Nicolini, *Aspetti della vita religiosa, politica e letteraria del Cinquecento* (Bologna, 1963); A. Rotondò, "La pratica nicodemitica," *Rivista Storica Italiana*, LXXIX (1967). For the relations between religion, morality, and literature, B. Croce, *Storia dell'età barocca in Italia* (2d ed., Bari, 1946), is still fundamental.

18. *Prose della volgar lingua*, bk. II, 20.

Index

Index

The Three Ages of
The Italian Renaissance
was composed, printed, and bound by
Kingsport Press, Inc., Kingsport, Tennessee.
The type is Granjon
and the paper is Simpson Lee's Vicksburg Vellum.
Design is by Edward G. Foss